Praise for *The* ~~Ugliest Word~~

In this aptly named book, Annie pulls back the curtain on a topic shrouded with shame and secrecy and begs the world to take a look. Her call for awareness reverberates through the souls of those affected by childhood sexual assault. To read this book is to catch a glimpse into the lives and hearts of so many children around the world.

—*Jessica Rose, host of the* Life After Trauma *podcast*

Once I started reading *The Ugliest Word*, I couldn't put it down. Annie Margis writes with a style that is so incredibly detailed yet flows so smoothly that I became fully immersed in the story of Lark, a bright, creative little girl with a terrible secret. The emotions this book wrung from me were astounding. By the end of the last page, I had tears in my eyes for a variety of reasons. For survivors of childhood trauma, for those who care about children, or for anyone with a strong sense of morality and a strong stomach, I can't recommend this book strongly enough!

—*Laine Hissett, podcast host*

The Ugliest Word is a poignant, riveting, and highly necessary book. Annie paints the family dynamics that set the stage for and normalize sexual abuse with stunning precision. This book is a must read if we are ever to end the scourge that is generational family trauma and abuse. I can't recommend it highly enough.

—*Peter Buecker, MD, host of* Unbroken: Reclaiming Your Self After Childhood Trauma *podcast*

The Ugliest Word is accurate. This book helps us understand the slow and methodical way perpetrators groom children and how deeply their acts embed on the self-concept and worldview of those subjected to this cruel and deeply personal offense.

—*Sherryll Kraizer, PhD, Safe Child Organization*

This book is a gift for anyone who has experienced incest as well as those ready to uncover the darkest family secret. Survivors who have long been ostracized, left to make sense of mystery illness and confront their horror alone, will find incredible healing and validation in *The Ugliest Word*. Annie Margis illustrates the resilient innocence of childhood that internalizes the abuse until it can no longer go unspoken and manifests itself years later. There were moments while reading that I thought, *Yes! This is a red flag!* The immature, unprovoked sexual comments that cause other adults to roll their eyes and force a laugh. The parent's inability to address serious topics with their own children. This book will sit you down and open the conversation that too many are uncomfortable to even begin. Thank you for writing *The Ugliest Word*!

—*Rebecca Garifo, author of* Too Sensitive: An Empath's Story
and host of the Empath's Alchemy *podcast*

The Ugliest Word has provided me with an intense and much-needed education in the area of childhood incest. If I was still teaching teenagers, many of whom have experienced childhood abuse, I would be so grateful to be able to share with them the valuable and meaningful message of *The Ugliest Word*.

—*Robin Trigg, teacher and author of*
I Am David, A Journey to the Soul of Autism

The Ugliest Word speaks the unspeakable. Lark's story is written with immense sensitivity and raw honesty. Incest is a deeply taboo subject but an all-too-common experience, and our collective silence perpetuates it. Annie Margis breaks that silence and bravely shines a light on one of the darkest human experiences.

—*Hecate F. Okay, host of* Finding OK, *a healing podcast for survivors of sexual assault and abuse*

In *The Ugliest Word*, author Anne Margis' generous use of dialogue is greatly appreciated. The quiet part, the silenced part, is given a voice. We survive abuse, and sometimes we live to tell the tale.

—*Tonya GJ Prince, WESurviveAbuse.com*

I could imagine myself in Lark's shoes, being bullied by her maternal figure only to be pushed to her abuser's grips. *Pedophile, incest, molestation*: These are all words that cannot keep being ignored. The writer exposed these in important ways through symbolism. This is a harsh reality that needs to be exposed. The writer is on the right path. Thank you for allowing me this opportunity.

—*Anne Marie Byzuk, podcast host*

Bravery at its best. A long overdue and much-needed look into the tragic world of incest abuse.

—*Pamela Clark, BCBA, LBA, host of* Deshaming *podcast*

This book put a splinter in my heart.

—*Chris, a survivor*

A bright, amiable girl suffers for years from her father's molestation in this novel. Five-year-old Lark Kurvas' life in the 1960s is far from ideal. Her mother, Hattie, drinks excessively and is brutally condescending. It's apparent her younger brother, Rex, gets preferential treatment, including his participation in baseball taking precedence over Lark's piano lessons. But most dreadful is her father, Scully, who habitually molests her—behavior Lark initially believes to be typical.

Margis' novel is unsurprisingly bleak. Her laconic prose, which makes the short book a quick read, also implies much of Scully's atrocities. Lark is certainly a tragic figure, but she's also an appealing character who aspires to be a writer and, despite relentless burdens, finds strength in herself. She still bears the incalculable repercussions of molestation, dealing with troubles, such as alcoholism, in later years.

A grim but important story that addresses a disturbing subject with intelligence and consideration.

—*Kirkus*

In this harrowing tale of childhood sexual abuse, Margis (*Say a Few Words*) shows how molestation can affect a survivor for her whole life. Lark Kurvas is a creative child, growing up with her family in 1950s California. Neglected by her mother in favor of her younger brother, she develops a close relationship with her father, Scully. But he manipulates her affection, repeatedly abusing and raping her throughout her childhood. Lacking companionship, Lark befriends the mysterious Glassman, an unknown person who leaves glass bottles and notes in her backyard. As an adult, Lark's healing is interrupted when she must decide whether to return home to see her dying father, despite his refusal to admit to his crimes.

The narrative is unsparing, and Margis brings unflinching insight into Lark's pain and distress. Readers will share Lark's anguish and cringe with her fear. This is not an easy book to read; it is incredibly graphic. Some survivors will find comfort in the familiarity of Lark's story, while others may find it too much like reliving their own pain. For readers who wish to learn more about the brutal reality of sexual abuse, the taboo surrounding incest, and the lack of support survivors often face, this challenging, gripping, and meaningful story is a must-read.

Takeaway: This haunting, closely told story of childhood sexual abuse will draw in survivors seeking affirmation and others looking for a survivor's-eye-view of devastating trauma.

—*BookLife*

THE UGLIEST WORD

Annie Margis

Published by
Impact Driven Publishing
3129 S. Hacienda Boulevard, Suite #658
Hacienda Heights, CA 91745

Manufactured in the United States of America, or in the United Kingdom when distributed elsewhere.

Margis, Annie
The Ugliest Word
LCCN: 2020904849
        ISBN: 978-1-7347528-0-9
        eBook: 978-1-7347528-1-6

Cover design: Natasha Clawson
Author photo: Annie Margis
Copyediting and interior design: Claudia Volkman

TheUgliestWord.com

They threw dirt on us, but we were seeds.

1

"Don't smile."

"I'm not smiling," says five-year-old Lark, trying hard not to.

"*Shh.* Don't say anything," Scully cautions.

He paints pink lipstick on his little girl's upper lip, then the lower one. He smears it a little.

"I'm not saying anything." Wearing her pink bathrobe, Lark stands on a child's step stool before the bathroom mirror. Scully's wrapped in a towel.

Scully erases the lipstick smear harshly with his thumb and then repaints the lower lip. It's a perfect Barbie-doll mouth.

"Now shut your eyes."

She squeezes her eyes closed as hard as she can. Scully pulls at the squinted skin of Lark's right eyelid, then brushes on sky-blue eye shadow.

"I have a surprise for you," he says.

"Is it a present?"

"How did you know?" Scully finishes with the right eye and begins to pull at her left eyelid.

"Is it a Barbie?" Lark asks.

"You have too many Barbies."

"Nobody has too many Barbies," Lark says.

"Don't talk, Goose. Keep your eyes closed."

"I'm not a goose. I'm a lark. You always forget." Scully brushes rouge on Lark's cheeks. Lark squirms with anticipation.

"Sit still."

"I can't wait. I hope it's a Barbie!"

"Five more seconds. Count backward."

"Five . . . four . . . two . . ."

Scully helps, saying, "Three."

"Three . . . four . . . now I'm all mixed up. Can't I count the regular way?"

"The magic won't work then," Scully insists. "Five . . ."

With an extravagant sigh, Lark goes back to counting, "Five . . ." but she can't help peeking at herself in the mirror. When she sees her reflection, her eyes open wide.

"You Barbied me!" she shouts. Lark is as delighted as only a five-year-old who believes she's Barbie can be. Then dropping her voice to its lowest volume, she adds, "Glassman will never rec'nize me now."

They hear the front door open and shut.

"Glassman!" Lark leaps into the bathtub and yanks the curtain closed.

But it's not Glassman. Hattie, Lark's mom, sings out like Desi Arnaz, "Scully, I'm hooome!"

"Mama!" Lark yelps, jerking the shower curtain open again. Scully tries to hold Lark back, but she runs off, out of the bathroom and down the hall. She smashes into Hattie, a tiny woman who looks too young to be Lark's mother. She's balancing Lark's two-year-old brother, Rex, on one hip. Lark hops around and around Hattie.

"Mama! Mama, look! Look, Mama! Mama! Mama! Mama!"

"What's on your face?" Hattie demands. Putting Rex down and digging a Kleenex out of her purse, she wipes off Lark's lipstick, smearing it around like a clown mouth. Scully steps out of the bathroom. He leans against the door frame, arrogant as James Dean. He needs a shave, but he's a charmer. When he leans over to kiss Hattie, she turns her head. His kiss lands on her ear.

"For God's sake, Scully! She's your daughter, not your doll." Hattie grips Lark roughly by the shoulder. "Come on, you need a shower."

Lark speaks carefully so as not to antagonize her mother. "I a'ready did. With Daddy."

"Well, you need another one." Hattie pushes past Scully and shoves Lark into the bathroom. Scully starts to follow them, but Hattie slams the door in his face. "I can't be gone five minutes without you causing trouble."

"I didn't mean to," Lark apologizes.

"I wasn't talking to you." Hattie pulls the door open again and sees Scully holding Rex. She grabs the toddler away. "Don't you ever touch my boy."

With an impish grin, Scully reaches over and musses Hattie's hair. "Don't you worry your pretty head."

2

On an overcast September day, a sugar maple in Lark's backyard dazzles with its sixty-four-crayon box of colored leaves. A swing set stands in the middle of the shaggy lawn, and a rusty incinerator hogs up a corner. A loose board in the back fence offers a view into the alley: an unpaved lane between the neighborhood's backyards, taboo turf.

Scully is shoveling maple leaves into the incinerator. Lark, wearing her pink overalls, lies in a pile of leaves and swooshes her arms around, making leaf angels. Scully flings a rake full of leaves into the air, and they rain down on her. She brushes them out of her face, pretending to drown. "Help! Help!" she says, laughing.

"Nyah-ha-ha!" Scully snickers diabolically, like Snidely Whiplash.

Through the hole in the alley fence, an eye peeks into the yard, blinks, and withdraws. Scully stops raking and glances at the fence just after the eye disappears, but he's sure he saw something.

"Hush a minute. *Shhh!*" he whispers. A pause, then, "Hear that?"

Lark shakes her head silently.

"When you don't hear anything, that's Glassman."

Lark covers her ears and whispers urgently, "I don't wanna hear Glassman."

"You won't hear him."

"Then how do you know when he's there?"

"You never know when he's there, so it seems like he's always there." Lark's pupils are huge. "Maybe he is."

After a weighted silence, Scully shouts. "Boo!"

Lark screams.

Scully drops the rake and kneels beside her. "Shush, Baby Bird! People gonna think I'm hurting you."

At first, Lark looks at Scully with terror. But then she throws her arms around his neck and clings. "I don't wanna hear Glassman."

"Don't worry," her father reassures her. "You won't hear him."

3

Lark's living room is decorated with what a "hip" insurance agent and a stay-at-home mom can afford in the 1960s. A gold plaster bust of President Kennedy sits on top of the black-and-white TV/record-player console. Palm fronds are tucked behind a Catholic crucifix on the wall above Kennedy.

Still in her pink overalls, Lark clings to her mother's leg as Hattie, with Rex in her arms, tries to exit through the front door. Scully stands by.

Lark begs, "Don't go, Mommy!"

"I have to go to church, Lark."

"I hate church."

"You do nothing of the kind."

"Chipper up, Baby Bat!" Scully interrupts as he peels Lark off her mother's leg and tosses her into the air. "When you gonna learn to fly?"

Hattie goes out the door. After a few test flights, Scully flies Lark into the bathroom. "You've got leaves in your ears."

"And in my mouth!" says Lark.

"Better wash it out with soap," Scully teases.

"Do I have to?"

"Absotively posilutely . . . not!" Scully runs the bathwater while Lark takes off her clothes. She gets into the tub.

"Put in some bubble bath, Birdie." Lark pours in way too much. Bubbles swell and overflow.

"*Mmm,*" Lark says, "smells like oranges." She scoops out some bubbles with her hand and licks them. "They don't taste orange."

"Don't eat the bubbles, Pigeon." Scully takes his clothes off and climbs into the tub.

"No, Daddy! You take up too much room."

"You fit between my legs."

"Last time the water overflowed, remember?"

Scully laughs.

4

In the bedroom she shares with Rex, Lark sits cross-legged on the edge of her bed in her robe as Scully, in his robe, sits on her little desk chair.

"I love you so much, Chickadee. I got you another present."

"Is it a Barbie?" she asks.

"You have too many Barbies," Scully teases, then simultaneously they proclaim, "Nobody has too many Barbies!"

"It's not a Barbie," Scully says. He hands Lark a diary.

"A book!" Lark cries.

"A special kind of book. It's a diary, for you to write your stories. As soon as you learn how to write."

"Oh, I know how to write. I just don't know how to put it down on paper yet."

"Look what I wrote on the first page." Scully points to the inscription. "'No one will ever love you like I do.' Like the song." He sings a little song. "No one will ever love you like I do . . ."

"Can I draw pictures in it?"

"You certainly may."

Lark digs her crayons out of a drawer and starts to draw her first depiction of Glassman: a stick man with a martini glass for a head and a sword made of a broken bottle.

"Daddy, have you ever seen Glassman?" she asks as she colors fiercely.

"Sure, lots of times."

"Can you draw a picture of him for me?" She offers him a crayon.

He takes the crayon, plays with it, bites on it, writes on his hand with it. "How do you make it work?" he finally asks.

"Daddy, you know how. Pretty please, Da-da?"

"You help me, then. Come sit on my lap."

5

Two years later

In Lark's living room, Scully and Hattie, both cheery with gin under their belts, preside over four-year-old boys in pirate hats and their parents with adult beverages in hand. Georgia O'Donnell, a pregnant African American woman, Lark's godmother and Hattie's best friend, has come to the party with her husband and two of her sons.

It's Lark's brother's fourth birthday party. Rex is dressed up as a pirate king with a crown.

Seven-year-old Lark, wearing a pink princess dress and her tiara, peeks around the doorjamb and signals Scully. He nods, claps his hands, and strikes a footman's pose.

"Ladies and gentlemen, may I have your attention? I'd like to introduce Princess Peacock." He draws out the word *Peeeecock* salaciously, winking at Georgia. She feigns a look of disgust, then rolls her eyes.

"No, Daddy, no! I'm Princess Lark!"

"My apologies, Princess Dark."

"*DADdeee!*" Lark gives up on Scully and sashays into the room.

Rex takes a pirate run at her and stabs her with his plastic sword. "No girls allowed!"

Other pirate boys lift their swords, too, and start to chant. "No girls allowed! No girls allowed!" The chant continues.

Georgia grabs her two sons and drags them back. "That's not good party manners," she scolds.

Hattie says, "Let 'em be. They're right." She glares at Lark. "Stop trying to corner all the attention, Lark."

Hattie tears the tiara off, ripping out some of Lark's hair in the process. She tosses it, and the tiara lands at Georgia's feet. Georgia picks it up.

Lark rubs the top of her head. Her eyes smart, but she'd die before she'd let Hattie see her cry. Scully lifts her up and positions her on his hip, then goes on with the spiel he's giving Georgia's husband.

"Say, O'Donnell, look who I've got here. Now, I've covered myself with life insurance for her, in case anything happens. You should have the same for Georgia and your crop of boys. Never know when the good Lord'll call us home, do we?" He sets Lark down and pats her on the behind.

Georgia corners Father Mulcahy, an Irish Catholic priest, same age as Scully. "Now come on, Father. Surely, you've wondered what it would be like to have a little boy of your own. I could give you one of mine. I've got plenty."

"All God's children are mine, Mrs. O'Donnell," Father Mulcahy says with a laugh.

"Someone to call you 'Daddy.'"

"They call me 'Father.'"

"I have to give you that." Georgia tallies up a point in the air. "But what about a wife? No woman to call you 'Honey'?"

"Have you had some of the punch?" Father Mulcahy dodges. "It socks a punch, so to speak."

"Don't I know it, running on as I am. My cup's empty. Would you do me the honor?"

Father Mulcahy bows and takes her cup, then walks away. He sees Lark's princess dress sticking out from under the punch table and pulls her out. "Hiding from the pirates, milady?"

"I hate Rex. Everybody loves him, and nobody loves me."

"Your family loves you more than anyone else ever will, except God."

Dubious, Lark asks, "Are you sure?"

"I'm sure."

She considers this a moment, then shakes her head. "I'm doomed."

Hattie spies Lark talking to Father Mulcahy and storms over. "Stop bothering Father. Go to your room. This isn't your party."

"Hattie," Father Mulcahy tries to intervene, but Hattie ignores him and drags Lark away. Rex crowds in on Lark.

"Your bedroom's the ocean, and the hallway is the plank."

Other pirates rally behind Rex, cheering, "Walk the plank! Walk the plank!"

Hattie lets go of Lark, and the boys start pushing her down the hall. They shove her into her room, where she sprawls.

"Aargh," Rex gargles. "You're doomed!" Lark kicks the door closed.

The boys stand outside the door, banging on it and chanting, "No girls allowed!" Rex shouts through the door, "You're drowning in the ocean now."

From inside her bedroom, Lark shouts back, "I'm a mermaid! I can breathe underwater."

Georgia walks down the hall holding Lark's tiara. She grabs hold of the collar of one of the pirates. "Go mutiny somewhere else," she says, knocking on Lark's door.

Lark responds, "No boys allowed."

"I don't think I'm a boy," Georgia says, patting her pregnant abdomen, "but I make no guarantees about my belly bun."

Georgia opens the door and walks into Lark's room. She shuts the door behind her.

"Does this lock?" she asks.

Lark grunts. "That would be cool. Fairy Godmother?"

"Yes, Fairy Goddaughter?"

"Why are boys so awful?"

"They're practicing to be husbands."

"I'm never going to get married," Lark states unequivocally.

"You'll become a nun then."

"No. I want to be a writer."

Georgia puts the tiara back on Lark. "All power to you," she says.

6

It's the first day of first grade. Lark is sitting with her father, mother, and brother in their 1960s-style kitchen. Booze bottles crowd the messy counter. Lark's wearing a Catholic school uniform: plaid skirt, white button-up shirt with short sleeves, and a beanie bobby-pinned to her hair.

"Now you behave yourself at school," Hattie warns Lark. "None of your nonsense. The nuns won't stand for it. They'll hit you with a ruler and make you stand in the corner."

"But I don't know how to be in first grade," Lark worries. "What am I supposed to do?"

Scully puts his hand over Lark's. "The nuns will tell you what to do."

"They don't take no malarkey, Irish nuns," Hattie warns.

Lark's eyes grow round. "I don't have 'nomalarkey.' I don't even know what 'nomalarkey' is."

"Fool," Hattie says. "It means doing something wrong."

"Like a sin?"

"Exactly like a sin."

"Now, Hattie, it isn't such a terrible sin to piss off a nun," Scully soothes. "I've done it myself."

"Scully! Watch your mouth!"

"You said 'malarkey.'"

"Not a four-letter word," Hattie snaps back.

"What if I do it by accident?" Lark asks her mom.

"Do what?"

"Piss off a nun."

Hattie turns red. "Now look what you've taught her. I won't be responsible if they throw her out of school on her first day."

Scully pets Hattie, calming her down. "Relax. You're frightening the child."

"Just telling her the truth. Preparing her for life," Hattie argues.

"Well, she's not going to be very prepared for life if she's too scared to start first grade."

Lark jumps in. "I'm not afraid of nothing."

Scully corrects her. "I'm not afraid of anything."

"I'm just like you!" Lark agrees.

7

In Lark's first-grade classroom, seven-year-old girls in uniforms like Lark's sit with their hands folded on top of their desks. Kathleen is one of the girls. She's blonde and freckled, with green cat eyes. Sister Magillicutty, an Irish nun wearing a black, floor-length habit and a white wimple, commands the room.

"I'm certain that not one young lady is crossing her ankles," Sister Magillicutty lies. A flurry of ankles uncross. "Young ladies sit with their feet flat on the floor, knees touching." Sister demonstrates by pulling an empty student desk up to the front of the class and sitting in it herself.

"We have to keep our knees together so boys can't look up our skirts," Lark says.

Sister Magillicutty tries to rise from the small student desk, but she's stuck. "Where did you hear such a thing?" she demands.

Proudly, Lark says, "My daddy taught me that."

"Go wash your mouth out with soap," the nun orders her. To Kathleen, she says, "Go with her. Make sure she obeys."

The two girls walk down the hall. Kathleen pushes open the door to a pink bathroom. The pink sinks and toilets are small and low to the floor.

Lark marvels, "Look at the color! Pink sinks! It's practically a poem. Pink sinks jinx Tink. Wink wink."

"They wanna make sure we're in the right bathroom," Kathleen says. "I peed in the boys' bathroom once."

"Did you die?"

"Yes."

Lark reluctantly walks to the sink and starts pumping powdered soap out of an aluminum dispenser screwed into the wall.

"You're not going to seriously do it? Wash your mouth with soap?"

"Sister told me to."

"Do you always do what you're told?"

Lark ponders this a moment, then says, "No, because my mom told me not to piss off a nun, and I guess I did that." Lark lifts a handful of powdered soap to her lips and opens her mouth.

Kathleen yells, "Stop!" She grabs Lark's hand and dumps out the soap, then rinses it off under the tap. She soaps up her own fingers so she has some bubbles. "Close your mouth," she says. Lark does what she's told. Kathleen paints bubbles around Lark's mouth and on her chin, like a bathtub Santa's beard.

"There," she says, admiring her handiwork. "Now let's go back." Kathleen opens the door and holds it for Lark to walk through. "Wanna be best friends?" she asks.

"Okay," Lark says. They shake pinkie fingers to seal the deal, then take each other's hands as they walk out of the bathroom and down the hallway.

Suddenly, a loud alarm starts blaring. Lark and Kathleen run back to their classroom.

"Girls! Girls! Quickly!" Sister Magillicutty is yelling. "Under your desks! Hands behind your necks. Make yourselves as small as you can." The nun watches as the first-graders climb under their desks and curl up. She walks around poking them with a ruler if their behinds are sticking out.

"Hail Mary full of grace, the Lord is with thee," she starts to pray. "Blessed art thou among women, and blessed is the fruit of thy womb. Now everybody . . ."

A few girls know the refrain to this prayer, but some don't. Lark knows it and says it out loud.

"Holy Mary, Mother of God, pray for us sinners, now and at the hour of our death."

"We'll have to work on that," Sister Magillicutty says. The alarm bell sounds three short blasts to end the drill.

"All right, girls. Get up and back in your desks. Everything's fine. It wasn't a real nuclear attack. Just a practice drill."

"What's a nuke-you-lar attack?" Kathleen asks.

"New-clee-er attack. Sister Mary Jean will explain it in social studies."

8

Scully is listening to the radio, sitting in the recliner in his man cave beside his stack of *Playboy* magazines and his gun collection. An open bottle of bourbon sits on his side table. Beer cans overflow the wastebasket. The man cave is in a corner of the garage, cordoned off by hanging sheets.

Lark stands next to the man cave and speaks through the sheet. "Knock, knock."

"Come in," Scully says.

"You're supposed to say, 'Who's there?'"

"But I know who's there."

"Just say 'Who's there?' please."

"Who's there, Sandpiper?"

"Orange."

"Orange who?"

"Orange you going to open the door?"

"There isn't any door." Scully opens the sheet and takes Lark's hand.

"Daddy! You're ruining my joke!"

"What did the zero say to the eight?"

"I don't know yet. It was only my first day."

Scully pauses for his punchline. "Nice belt."

"Daddy, I like first grade."

"I like that you like first grade." Scully pulls her all the way into the man cave.

"What's a nuke-lee-ar attack?" she asks.

Scully is enthusiastic. "That's when we blow Russia to kingdom come."

"Where's kingdom come?"

"Ask your teacher. She's a nun, right?"

"Sister Magillicutty. She says I have to have a sin so I can make my First Confession."

"Never do wrong and you'll never need to confess."

"Is anything I do a sin?"

"Who told you to ask that?" Scully demands.

"Sister Magillicutty."

"Why would she tell you that? What did you say?"

"Nothing."

"Never say nothing to nuns."

"Anything. Daddy, can my new best friend spend the night?"

Scully relaxes. "Sure. *Mi casa es tu casa.*"

"What?"

"Yes."

"Yes? It means yes?"

"Si."

"Yes! I'll tell her at school tomorrow. Can she come home with me on Friday? It's not a school night."

"Supercali-absolutely." Scully picks up Lark and puts her on his lap. "Let's play horsey. Giddy-up."

9

Lark and her seven-year-old friends, Lynn and Kathleen, are in Lark's backyard, taking turns peeking into the alley through the loose board in the decrepit back fence. Lark is lecturing. "The Aluminum Ladies who collect the cans, they sound like metal—*pop*, like when Dad dents his beer cans—and you have plenty of time to hide. But Glassman? You never hear him."

"I've seen Glassman," Kathleen says.

"No, you haven't," Lynn argues.

"Yes, I have. He's made of glass."

"No, he isn't, because I've seen Glassman," Lynn says.

"No, you haven't."

"Yes, I have, and he's got a patch over one eye!"

"And a wooden leg?" Lark breaks into the argument.

"Nah, that's a pirate," Kathleen says.

Lark leaps up, excited by an idea. "Let's play pirates!"

"That's a boy game," Lynn says. "We can't play a boy game."

"Okay," Lark continues, "I've got a better idea! Let's put on a play!"

Kathleen is on board. "A play about pirates!"

Lynn whines, "We don't have any boys."

"I've got a better idea," Lark says. "We'll do Cinderella!"

"I have the dress!" Lynn and Kathleen shout together.

They eye one another suspiciously. Lark decides, "Cinderella and the Pirate King!" They play sword-fight with each other.

Moments later, Lark, Kathleen, and Lynn peek from behind the hallway door into the garage and at the man cave in the corner. The girls hear a ball game playing on the radio from behind the sheets.

Lark whispers to Lynn, "You go ask him. He won't say no to a guest."

"I'm not a guest," Lynn says. "I live next door. Kathleen's the guest."

Lark turns to Kathleen. "Go on," she urges. Kathleen looks doubtful, then walks across the garage and starts to pull aside a sheet and enter the man cave. Lark rushes to her side and pulls the sheet back down. "Wait! I mean, don't actually go inside! Just talk through the sheet!"

Too late. Scully has seen Kathleen, and he lifts the sheet himself. "Well look who's here? Who are you?"

Kathleen replies, "I'm Lark's friend."

"You're lucky to have such a friend," Scully says.

"Thank you."

"How can I help you, Friend of Lark?" he asks.

Kathleen explains, "Lark's written a play."

"I'm sure she has," Scully says proudly. "And you're her literary agent?"

Kathleen looks confused. "She told me I was the producer."

"Producer, huh? That's like being God. Executive producer? Or real producer?"

"I think I'm real. I'm not sure. It's my first job."

Lynn signals from across the garage, stage-whispering, "*Psst!* Ask him!"

Lark nods and gestures to go ahead.

Kathleen screws up her courage. "We need a pirate king."

Lynn yells across the garage, "For our play!"

"There's nothing I like better than playing with little girls," Scully says, getting up from his chair. Lark is ecstatic.

"So, I'm to be the pirate king, am I? Always knew I had royal blood. Who's the director? Yoo-hoo! Direct me!"

Lark says, "I'm the director."

"You write and direct your own productions, do you?" Scully asks, impressed. "You star in them too?"

"Yes."

"Naturally. So, what's your play about?"

"Daddy, you know Cinderella. You read it to me a million times."

"Used to be your favorite."

"Only instead of Cinderella being human, she's a bird."

"She's a bird?"

Lark says, "It was an evil spell that made her a bird."

"Cast by her evil stepmother," Lynn elaborates the plot.

"Of course," Scully nods.

"But you, the pirate king, are going to marry the bird so she can turn back into a princess."

"I'm going to, am I? Usually the man asks. What about your brother, Rex?"

"He refuses to play with us." The group walks out of the garage and into the backyard. A pink blanket hangs over the swing set to form the curtain of Lark's outdoor theater.

Lark directs Scully. "So, Daddy, please pay attention. At first, you have to be the ocean. That's at the beginning when we are on the ship, which is in front of the curtain, see? The teeter-totter is the plank. Then later you're the king."

"How will I know which to be when, ocean or king?"

"This is only the dress rehearsal right now, so I'll give you a clue when it's your turn to do something."

"You mean a 'cue'?"

"No, Daddy, a clue. It's theater talk."

"Why can't one of your little friends be the pirate king?"

"They're *girls!*" Lark sends Scully a look of utter disbelief that he couldn't see something so plain. "Besides, I wrote the part for you." Lark hands Scully the hose, then goes to turn it on. Kathleen begins her spiel, "Ladies and gentlemen."

Lynn tugs on Scully's sleeve and tells him, "I'm Cinderella."

Lark disagrees. "No, you're not! You're the wicked step-mother. I'm Cinderella."

Lynn puts on her pout face and offers an ultimatum. "I'm Cinderella, or I won't be in your stupid play."

Scully stage-whispers to Lark, "Diva."

Lark repeats the word. "Diva! It's my backyard, and he's my dad, so I'm Cinderella." Lynn glares at Lark, who ignores her dramatics.

"Then I'll be the wickedest stepmother who ever lived," Lynn huffs.

Scully pats Lynn on the back and says, "Good for you."

Lark pushes Lynn away from her dad, while Kathleen climbs the teeter-totter as if it were a crow's nest. With an imaginary spyglass, she looks out upon the far horizon. "There aren't any ladies and gentlemen out there."

"After dress rehearsal we'll go out and get people to come, right, Daddy?" Lark calls from the water faucet as she turns it on.

"That's what you gotta do, drum up business." Scully mimes rat-a-tatting with both hands at the very moment the water squirts out of the hose. He gets Lynn and Kathleen soaking wet. Kathleen screams happily, but Lynn isn't sure she's having fun, so Scully hands her the hose so she can squirt him back.

"We'll have to change this play to Moby Dick," Scully

says, laughing. "Lark can be the captain going down with the ship."

Lark tries to tug the hose away from Lynn, getting soaked in the process. "How 'bout Cinderella gets kidnapped by pirates, and the pirate king saves her? That's the way I wrote it."

Scully acts like he doesn't hear her. "Take off your wet things, and we'll hang them on the bushes to dry. Then we'll play Nymphs in the Fountain."

The girls remove some of their wet clothing. "Can I leave my panties on?" Kathleen asks.

Scully says, "May you?"

"Yes, I may," Kathleen answers.

The girls all leave their underwear on. Still fighting over the hose, Lynn squirts Scully, getting his shirt wet. Scully takes it off. "Now, my little nymphs, under the waterfall."

In the living room window that looks out on the yard, the curtain lifts, then silently drops back down.

10

Using fallen branches and her pink theater curtain, Lark has constructed a hideaway among some bushes in the backyard. She's sitting cross-legged in there, learning cat's cradle solitaire from a book. She keeps making mistakes, but she tries again and again until she gets it right.

She hears a noise. "Glassman," she breathes, and curls into a fetal position.

But it's only Hattie, humming as she skips gaily out of the house, across the yard, and to the alley gate. She opens it and calls into the alley. "Come! Come! Come in!"

Lark can't maintain her fetal position. She's too curious to see what Hattie is doing. Two tiny Japanese women appear at the gate. The Aluminum Ladies! Wearing traditional clothes, the women ply the alley collecting discarded cans in their beat-up Radio Flyer wagon. Hattie has something in her hand, something she wants to give them.

"Close your eyes," Hattie tells them. The women don't understand. "Close your eyes," she repeats, louder. She squeezes her own eyes shut, waits a second, then opens her eyes only to see the women squinting at her.

"No, no," Hattie says. They back away. Hattie is scaring them. She touches her index fingers to the eyelids of one lady. "Close your eyes." They finally get it, and both close their eyes. "For you, from me," Hattie says as she puts a necklace around the neck of each. The necklaces are made of beer can pull-tabs folded over one another into chains.

Aluminum Lady One spies Lark peeking through the bushes. "Smash cans, little girl?" she invites Lark. "Come. Come. Smash cans."

Aluminum Lady Two fishes a Coors can out of her wagon, then smashes it with her tiny foot. It makes the most satisfying sound. "Come in! Come in!" she calls Lark.

Hattie sing-songs, "Come out, come out, wherever you are." They all encourage Lark, but she won't come out of the bushes. Hattie apologizes. "She's an idiot." The Aluminum Ladies bow deeply and move off down the alley. Hattie closes the gate, then jerks Lark out of her hideaway.

"You'd try the patience of a saint, and I ain't no saint. Why do you have to embarrass me?"

"I was afraid they would steal me."

"Why would they want you?"

"Because they're Alley People."

"Don't be prejudiced," Hattie scolds. "You think you're better than they are?"

"No. Why did you give them those necklaces?"

Hattie enters the house. "I thought they would like them," she says.

11

Two years later

Nine-year-old Lark sings as she whisks a cotton rag around the living room, dusting the furniture. She's making a game of it, singing to the knickknacks. As she swirls, she picks up the golden plaster bust of President John F. Kennedy from atop the new spinet piano and dances with him to the music of her own singing. She sets him on the piano bench and sits down next to him, then proceeds to dust off each key, one at a time, two at a time, triplets, then arpeggios, until a song emerges and her fingers burst into Chopin. She's no prodigy, but she plays by heart and plays well.

Hattie walks in with Rex and catches Lark having fun. "If I'd have known you'd play the dad-blasted piano day and night, I would've never let your dad rent the thing."

Lark spins around on the piano bench and sends John F. Kennedy flying. He shatters on the floor. Hattie makes the Sign of the Cross. "Mother of Mercy, pray for us."

Lark falls to her knees and tries to stick Kennedy's broken pieces back together.

Hattie shouts, "You'd try the patience of a saint. And I . . ." Hattie and Lark finish the phrase together, ". . . ain't no saint!" Hattie finds this funny, and her mood improves.

Tentatively, Lark hazards, "I looked it up. There is no Saint Hattie."

"Hattie stands for Hathor, Egyptian goddess. My mother was a heathen. When I married your father, he made me change my name, so I go by Hattie."

Lark says, "And there's no Saint Lark."

"Your father named you Lark. I gave you your middle name: Anne. Saint Anne." Together, Hattie and Lark intone, "Grandmother of God." They both find this funny.

"You'll need a confirmation saint name eventually," Hattie says. "Have I ever told you mine?"

"No." Lark is starting to enjoy this brief moment of friendliness from her mother.

"Guess."

"Guess what?"

"Fool. Guess my confirmation name."

Lark smiles at the game. "What does it start with?"

"That would make it too easy."

Lark guesses. "Mary? Mother of God?"

"No. It starts with a 'D.'"

"Diane?"

"Greek goddess of the forest. Or Roman. Never could tell the difference. Guess again."

"Daphne?"

"What are you, obsessed with heathen goddesses?"

"Those are the only 'D' names I know."

Hattie's bored with the game. "Dymphna. That's my confirmation name."

"Sounds like a nymph."

"She was a martyr," Hattie emotes, "like me."

Rex runs to the piano and starts banging on the keys. Lark's moment with her mother is shattered. The sound hurts Lark's ears. She sets down pieces of Kennedy and puts her hands over Rex's hands to show him how to be more gentle.

Hattie bristles. "Leave him alone. You're not the only one with talent. Come, follow me." She heads down the hall. Lark lets Rex's hands go, and none too willingly follows her mother.

12

Moments later, Hattie turns in at her own bedroom, which is
off-limits to Lark. She stops at the doorjamb and watches her
mother.

"I want to give you something," Hattie calls over her
shoulder as she opens her bottom drawer. She pulls out a pink
satin jewelry box. She turns and sees that Lark hasn't come into
the room yet. "It's all right, just this time. Here, take this from
me and set it on the bed."

Lark does what she's told. She sets the pink satin box on the
unmade bed and stands above it.

"Sit! Sit!" Hattie waves at her with rare joviality. Lark slowly
lowers herself down beside the jewelry box, hands folded in
her lap, eyes on the floor.

Hattie makes herself comfortable on the other side of the
jewelry box. "Isn't this fun?" she asks Lark. Lark nods, but she
doesn't look up. Hattie doesn't notice. When she opens the lid
of the box, a plastic ballerina in a taffeta tutu pops up and starts
twirling.

Lark reaches out to touch the tiny doll, but then pulls her
hand back. A music box begins to tinkle.

"I know that song!" Lark hums the tune along with the box.
"Chopin's 'Lullaby'! I can play that!" Hattie hums along too,

off-key, as she stirs pieces of costume jewelry around in the box with her pointer finger. Lark peeks inside the box.

"I like the colors on that one."

"You're an old-fashioned girl! Those were my grand-mother's." Hattie pulls the beads out. "From the Roaring Twenties. Try 'em on."

"Are you sure?"

"I said, try 'em on." As reluctantly as if it were a noose, Lark slips the necklace around her neck.

"Stand up!" her mother commands with a wide smile. Lark leaps to attention. "Look at that!" Hattie points at Lark's knees. The colorful beads hang past them. "That's how long they wore them back then. Fun, huh?"

"I could jump rope in this!" Lark takes hold of the necklace with both hands and bends her knees as if to jump. She glances up at Hattie, who's still grinning.

"You could, but don't. Sit down."

Hattie lifts a bracelet from the box. It's tarnished almost black. One charm hangs from it. "My charm bracelet."

"What's the charm, Momma? I can't tell."

"Betty Boop! An old cartoon character. Scully and I got married at a chapel in Hollywood, and he bought me this for a wedding present. Said he would buy me a new charm every time we went to a new place for a vacation. See? I only have the one charm."

Hattie slips the charm bracelet onto her own wrist. Betty dangles.

Back to the box, Hattie takes out a chain with a medal on it, both tarnished. "Here it is: my Saint Dymphna holy medal. I want you to wear it. Maybe she'll do you more good than she ever did me." Hattie lays the necklace on Lark's knee. "She's like a guardian saint."

Lark lifts the oval medal and fingers its surfaces. The metal is worn down. She can barely make out the image of a beheaded girl.

"My mother gave it to me when I got my period. She said her mother gave it to her. So now it's time to hand it down to you." Hattie takes the medal and puts it around Lark's neck. It hangs next to the gaudy twenties beads and seems to shame them.

"So it was your mom's medal? I mean, did she wear it?"

"Yes, and her mother before her. I don't know how far it goes back, but it's real silver, so you better not lose it."

"Cross my heart and hope to die, Momma, I'll never take it off."

"My father gave me this jewelry box," Hattie muses. Her eyes soften, then begin to glower. She closes the box. The music stops.

"I never knew your dad." Lark hints. "Will you tell me about him?"

"No. Better to let sleeping dogs lie."

13

From the hallway in the back of the house, Scully climbs a ladder and opens a trap door to the attic. He backs down the ladder and waves at Lark to go up. She sticks her head up into the attic and gazes around in awe before she climbs up the rest of the ladder. Scully climbs up behind her.

Scully has fixed up the attic for Lark. Pink taffeta hangs from the ceiling and drapes over her headboard. Pink roses stand in a vase on Lark's dresser, and rose petals and a chocolate bar lie on her pillow. Scully sings, "Happy birthday to you. You live in the zoo. You look like a monkey . . ."

"Is this for me?"

". . . and you smell like one too." They laugh. "I thought it was about time you had a room of your own."

"No more stinky Rex! Daddy, I don't know what to say."

"Say, 'I love you, Daddy.'"

Lark throws her arms around Scully's neck. "I love you, I love you, I love you, I love you!" Scully, with Lark around his neck, falls back onto Lark's bed.

They hear a crash downstairs.

"Glassman!" Lark dives under her desk.

"You don't have to hide, Goldfinch. It's probably only the Aluminum Ladies, and they don't steal little girls."

Not reassured, Lark huddles under her desk. From the kitchen, Hattie yells, slurring, "Lark!" Lark flinches. "Come here and sweep up this mess!"

Scully helps Lark up. "Better do what you're told."

Hattie sits at the kitchen table with a martini glass in her hand. Six-year-old Rex sits at the table, too, eating ice cream. A vodka bottle has fallen to the floor and shattered. Glass has splattered everywhere and crunches under Lark's feet. She shakes her head to get rid of the vodka fumes.

"Where were you?" Hattie demands.

Afraid to lie, Lark tells her. "Under my desk."

"Wastrel. I'll give you a reason to hide. Clean this up."

Lark carefully picks up pieces of glass and puts them in a brown paper sack that's already almost full of booze bottles.

"And take the garbage out to the incinerator. You're old enough to light a fire." She pauses to look Lark up and down. "How old are you now, anyway?"

"It's my birthday."

"I didn't ask what day it is. I asked how old you are."

"Nine." Lark isn't sure she's old enough to light the incinerator, but she stoically presses on. "Matches?" Hattie points to a kitchen drawer. Lark finds a box of stick matches in it.

Out in the backyard, Lark carries the garbage bags to the incinerator. She opens the lid and unceremoniously throws in the trash, then starts taking bottles out of the brown paper bag and throwing them in. She's about to toss in a frosted white glass bottle, but she notices that it still has liquor in it. She opens the bottle and chugs the liquor down. She sputters and wipes her mouth on her arm. It doesn't look like it's the first drink she's ever taken.

She lights a match and drops it into the incinerator, then

jumps back. The garbage bursts into flames that spew out, shooting up toward the sky.

14

The next day, humming Chopin, Lark approaches the incinerator, cold and silent now. She's brought with her an ash bucket and a hand shovel. She opens the lid on the front of the incinerator, and ashes spill out. She sputters with the dust and pulls her shirt up so it covers her mouth and nose, then excavates the ashes.

Lark's shovel hits something hard. She reaches in and pulls out a dusty glob of melted, many-colored glass. Sooty-faced and dusty-handed, Lark runs into the house to show her dad the blob of glass. She runs full-on into Hattie.

"Where are you going?"

Lark tries to hide the glass blob behind her back. "To my room."

"What's that dirty thing you've got in your hands?" Lark slowly draws the glass blob from behind her back. "You better pray Glassman doesn't find out you've melted his glass. No telling what he'll do." With a melodramatic tilt of her hip and shake of her finger, Hattie warns, "When my granny was little, the girl next door disappeared."

"Where did she go?" Lark asks.

"Glassman stole her."

"What did he do with her?"

"Took her to Glassland, probably. Who knows what happened there."

A dreamy look crosses Lark's face as she imagines a land made of glass. She whispers, "Glassland."

"They never found her."

"Maybe she's still there," Lark says. "In Glassland."

Hattie makes a witchy face and hisses, "She may be here, and she may be there, and she may be ev-er-y, ev-er-y-where."

"I thought that was Glassman."

"Don't talk back to me. Stand up straight. Get your hair out of your eyes."

"I want to go to Glassland. Do you think he'll kidnap me?"

"One can only hope." Hattie waves Lark off. Lark goes up to her attic room. She pulls out her diary to write a letter.

Dear Glassman,
  I melted your glass. I'm sorry. Here it is.
  I hope you can still use the blob for something.
  I think it's pretty.
Yours truly,
Lark Kurvas

Lark tears out the page and puts the diary away in its hidden nook. She folds the letter. Moments later, she stands outside Scully's man cave and speaks through the sheet.

"Daddy?"

"Yes, Flamingo?"

"I'm not a flamingo. You always forget. I'm a lark."

Scully pulls the sheet back. "Why it's you, Lark! I thought it was the flamingo!"

"We don't have a flamingo."

Scully is flabbergasted. "No? Well we certainly should. No flamingo? Imagine that!"

"Daddy, do you have an envelope?"

"An envelope. Did you ask your mother?" Lark looks at him like he's nuts. Of course she didn't ask Hattie.

"Oh, right. Best not to disturb the queen. But I fear I do not have an envelope, Sandpiper."

Lark spies an envelope sticking out of Scully's stack of *Playboy* magazines. "I see one! Right there!" She goes to pull the envelope out, but Scully stops her. He carefully pulls it out himself. It's a *Playboy* subscription envelope.

"This one already has writing on it," Scully says.

"That's okay. I'll just cross it off. Do you have a pen?" Scully gives her a black marker. "Perfect," she says. She puts her letter inside the envelope, then crosses off the *Playboy* address and writes GLASSMAN in big letters. She tapes the envelope to the blob of glass.

"Where'd you get this?" Scully asks, taking the blob of glass from Lark.

"I accidentally created it. I think it's kinda neat, but I'm giving it to Glassman."

Lark carries the blob of glass and the envelope out to the backyard. She can't bring herself to open the gate, so she goes to the loose board in the fence and sets the blob of glass down on the alley side.

The next day, up in her bedroom, Lark examines her bottle collection. She glances out the window and sees a glint of light beside the loose board in the fence. She can't tell what it is, but she makes her way to the attic trapdoor right away.

Lark races across the backyard. On her side of the board, she sees a bottle. The label reads "Bols Apricot Brandy." A ballerina stands in the center of the bottle. On the bottom, a key to wind it up. It plays "Blue Danube." She picks up the envelope. "Glassman" is crossed off, and "Lark Kurvas" is written across it. She opens it, then reads the letter.

Miss Lark,
   Thank you for the melted glass. It's a work of art.
   Here's a ballerina bottle for you in trade.
   I hope you like it.
Glassman

Lark hugs the ballerina bottle to her heart. "I have a friend!"

15

Wearing her Catholic school uniform, Lark pushes open the glass door of Mr. Evanko's Music Studio and Store. The brass temple-bells hanging on the door tinkle. Mr. Evanko's wife is working behind the counter. From the back room, a piano student labors through Chopin's "Lullaby."

"Hi, Lark!" Mr. Evanko's wife says cheerily.

"Hi."

"How was school?"

"Hmmm."

"Been better?" Mr. Evanko's wife asks.

"I got a 92 on my geography test."

"Congratulations."

"I missed the question about Gabon."

"What's Gabon?"

"That's what I said! Turns out it's a country on the equator. Now I remember. But the test is already over. I can't go back and change things." Lark seems heartbroken over this.

Mr. Evanko's wife commiserates. "I didn't know what Gabon was either, and I've made it through life all right this far." Lark picks up a piece of music and fondles it.

"Isn't 92 percent an A?" Mr. Evanko's wife won't drop the subject.

"Jane got a 98."

"What did she miss?"

"She put Wales in the Pacific Ocean."

Mr. Evanko's wife is puzzled. "Aren't there whales in the Pacific Ocean?"

Lark laughs. "Country Wales, not *whales* whales. Homonyms."

The background piano lesson ends. Mr. Evanko opens the studio door and ushers out his student.

"You're doing great, Bobby. Now I expect you to practice thirty minutes every day until I see you again."

Bobby sullenly replies, "Yeah, right."

"And next time your "Lullaby" will be so lovely, you'll put me to sleep."

"Yeah, right."

Lark pushes past them into the studio. She hurriedly sits down at the piano and plays Chopin's "Lullaby" perfectly. When finished, she lays her hands in her lap. "There."

Mr. Evanko comes in.

"Where?"

"I couldn't leave that guy's mangled Chopin hanging in the air. I had to erase it."

"You play beautifully." Lark makes a quick, jerky bow from the piano bench. "Listen, Lark, I have some bad news. Your father only paid me through last week, so we don't actually have a lesson today."

"Can't you put it on his tab?"

"What do you know about tabs?"

"I've been to the bar with my dad."

"Well, it isn't that he's paying me later. He canceled your lessons." This doesn't sink in at first. Then, when Lark realizes what Mr. Evanko means, she looks at him aghast.

"April Fool's!"

"I'm afraid not."

Lark puts her fingers resolutely on the keys and pounds out the opening of Chopin's "Funeral March."

"Musical humor. *Brava*, little Lark!" Mr. Evanko claps.

"I don't care!" Lark rages. "I don't need more lessons! I can read music now. I can play any song in the universe now. No one can take that away from me."

"That's the spirit, Lark!"

"How much do lessons cost? I'll get a job."

He calculates in his head, then offers her a discount. "Five dollars a month."

"A fortune!" Lark says. "But I could earn that somehow. I know how to do a lot of things."

Mrs. Evanko knocks at the studio door, then opens it. "I'm terribly sorry, Lark. Mr. Evanko, your 3:30 is here."

With mournful anger, Lark grabs her school satchel and storms out.

16

Lark stands outside Scully's man cave. "Daddy?"

"Who's there?" Scully calls.

"Daddy!"

"Daddy's there?"

Lark lifts the sheet. "It's me, Daddy."

"Puffin, is that you?"

"Daddy, be serious."

"I will not!" He takes Lark's hand, pulling her onto his lap.

"Daddy, I need money."

"Money, eh? Gotta earn that. How much you need?"

"Five dollars."

"That's a wad of cash. You think you can earn that much? What are you going to do?"

"Whatever you want."

"Is this about your music lessons?"

"Mr. Evanko said you weren't going to pay for them anymore."

"I wish I could, Nuthatch, but your mother holds the purse strings in this family." Scully holds on to her arm, but she gets up off his lap and goes out of the man cave.

17

Lark is in her bedroom, writing to Glassman.

Dear Glassman,
 I love my ballerina music box.
 I know it's really a liquor bottle in disguise.
 Kind of like a clue in a Sherlock Holmes story.
 I've read them all—have you?
 I could loan you a book.

She hears the doorbell ring but ignores it. Then she hears a commotion in the living room. She carefully hides her unfinished letter, then climbs down the ladder. Lark walks into the living room to discover two moving men wrapping her piano in quilts.

"I'm still playing that," Lark tells them.

"Sorry, kid," a moving man says.

Hattie flirts, cooing sweetly, "Don't bother the nice men, Lark. They're working."

Lark asks, "Why is my piano leaving?"

"It's not your piano," Hattie whispers meanly. "It's the store's piano. We were just renting it."

The moving men take the piano out of the house and down

the sidewalk to their truck. Lark walks backward ahead of them with her arms outstretched to impede their progress. Hattie follows.

"But," Lark argues, "you always liked it when I played Chopin, remember?"

"We can't afford it. Rex is playing Little League now, and that's expensive."

"I'll get a job!"

The moving men load the piano onto the truck. Lark kicks the ground, tearing a hole in the grass. Then she leans down and pats the grass back in.

Back in her room, she opens her dresser drawer and takes out a torn knitted sweater. She unravels the yarn and breaks it into different lengths, not using a scissors, but pulling hard on it until it snaps.

She starts picking up bottles from her shelves and from the floor, looking at each one, evaluating it for her project, then either putting it back down or setting it on the windowsill. She takes down the curtain rod over her window and removes the curtain from it, then puts the rod back up. Tying a length of yarn to each chosen bottle neck, she throws the yarn over the curtain rod and ties on that end of the yarn too. She hangs bottles on the curtain rod at different levels. The afternoon sun catches in the bottles and throws colors across Lark's face.

She steps back to admire her handiwork, then picks up a spoon from a used plate on the floor and hefts it, testing for weight. It seems right, so she tentatively tings the spoon against one bottle. A soft sound is emitted. She strikes other bottles with the spoon, and soon she is playing music.

18

Lark is tossing a bag of garbage into the incinerator when she notices a bundle sitting by the loose board in the fence. She hurries over to it and picks it up. There's an envelope. She opens it.

Dear Miss Lark,
  Your bottles in the window look like church glass.
  I found this bottle, and I thought you might like it.
Glassman

Lark unwraps the bundle to reveal a ceramic turkey with the label "Wild Turkey." She shakes it and listens: it's not empty. She pulls the cork and takes a swig. She grimaces, then sighs. With the Wild Turkey bottle in hand, Lark tries to sneak past Hattie, who's in the kitchen, but Hattie catches her. Hattie grabs the Wild Turkey bottle away from Lark.

"Well, Merry Thanksgiving!" Hattie uncorks the turkey bottle, sniffs it and takes a swig. "Where'd you get Wild Turkey?"

Lark says, "Glassman." Hattie snorts in disbelief. Lark heads for her ladder and climbs up. Hattie follows her all the way up the ladder and into the attic.

"The alley Glassman? I told you to beware of Alley People."

She throws herself like a dying ballerina onto Lark's bed. Lark really hates that. It means a booze-breath story that'll drag on forever. It also means Lark's bedspread will smell like Hattie's perfume.

Hattie hides her face in Lark's pillow, then she sniffs it and grimaces. "If you go any longer without changing your sheets, they're gonna look like the Shroud of Turin," she laughs. Lark fakes a smile. Hattie isn't satisfied with just a smile: she expected a laugh. She tosses the pillow at Lark's head. She's left a lipstick stain on it. "There. Don't ever say I never kissed ya." She tips the Wild Turkey one more time to see if it's empty. It is now. It won't be long before the liquor flips her switch and she starts yelling.

Hattie handles the bottles hanging in the window. She lifts one bottle and reads the label. "Azalea Tequiliana."

Lark doesn't like Hattie touching her bottles, so she tries to distract her. "I decided Azalea Tequiliana would be a great pen name for a murder mystery," she says. "So I wrote one."

"Did you kill me?" Hattie asks.

"Read it and see."

"Give it to your father. He'd love to read it. You better pray Glassman doesn't see those bottles hanging here. No telling what he'd do."

"No telling," Lark echoes, suppressing a smirk.

Hattie climbs down the ladder, leaving Lark alone at last. Lark settles down to write a letter.

Dear Glassman,
  Thank you for the glass bottles you leave me by the fence.
  The Wild Turkey is my new favorite one.
  That's some powerful drink. Have you tried it?
  Here's a Sherlock Holmes book for you.

I've already read it, so you can keep it.
Sincerely yours,
Lark

Lark takes down a volume of Sherlock Holmes stories and tucks the letter inside, with the words *Dear Glassman* sticking out.

19

Lark walks home from school a little faster than usual. She enters the house and walks right through it and out the back door, straight toward the loose board in the fence. Sure enough, something is there. No bottle. Just a note.

Dear Miss Lark,
    Don't be drinking Wild Turkey.
    You'll get me lynched.
Glassman

Lark laughs out loud. She runs into the house and scurries up the attic ladder to her room. Lark takes the pen from the pen holder on her desk—a small bottle—and tears out the last blank page of her journal and writes back.

Dear GM,
    I've been drinking since I could crawl up on my dad's lap
    and polish off his margaritas. I'd lick the salt off.
Cheers!
Lark

20

Scully, Rex, Lark, and her best friend Kathleen are finishing dinner at the kitchen table. Hattie is removing dinner plates and setting down dessert plates.

"Chocolate cream pie for dessert," she sings.

Rex says, "My favorite."

"I know," Hattie says. She sets a plate of pie down in front of everyone but Lark. She sets down one for herself on the kitchen counter and begins to eat it standing up.

"What's the buzz?" Scully asks. "Where's Ladybird's pie?"

"I don't want any," Lark lies.

"She's been putting on weight," Hattie says.

"She has not!" Scully grips the table edge.

"I have, Daddy; I'm fat. Besides, I really don't want my piece of pie."

"I'll eat hers," says Rex.

Kathleen has been watching this with visual trepidation.

"Eat, Lady Kathy, eat," Scully encourages her. Reluctantly, she eats her pie.

After dinner, Lark and Kathleen sit together on Lark's bed. Lark is flipping through one of her old diaries, stopping at each page that has a drawing of Glassman and showing it to Kathleen. On the first page is a stick figure with multicolored glitter glued over it, like a broken rainbow.

"I've seen Glassman, and he doesn't look like that," Kathleen pronounces.

"I was five. And no, you haven't."

"Where's his wooden leg?"

"He doesn't have a wooden leg." Lark turns the page. The next picture is of a two-dimensional gingerbread man with spiky skin that could cut. He's missing a leg.

"This one isn't finished," Lark says. "I remember—Daddy interrupted me."

"No, it is finished! It proves he's missing a leg."

"Which is not the same thing as having a wooden leg," Lark says with finality. She turns the page.

On the next page of the diary, there's a picture cut out of a comic book and glued in, a character made of clear glass so images warp as they reflect off him. Kathleen is impressed. "Wow! Did you draw this?"

"Of course I did. Not."

"I didn't know Glassman was a superhero!"

Lark says, "If he touches something, it turns to glass."

"For reals?"

Lark points out the Wild Turkey bottle. "That used to be a real turkey until Glassman touched it."

Kathleen caresses the bottle. "Gobble, gobble." Lark puts it back on its shelf. Kathleen picks up the ballerina bottle. "You gonna tell me this used to be real too?"

"Glassman turns people into glass, too, like Sodom and Gomorra."

"Maybe we could get him to touch Sister Saint Peter," Kathleen muses.

"I'll ask next time I see him."

"You've never seen him," Kathleen challenges. Lark

ignores her and turns to the next picture, drawn when she was older: Lark has colored the rays of Glassman's halo silver to look like broken glass and given him glass fingernails. Lark scowls at this image and hurriedly turns the page to show Kathleen the next one, but Kathleen turns the page back and laughs.

"He kind of looks like your dad."

"Does not."

"For reals."

"My dad's handsomer than that."

"Then why'd you make his hair like that? Just like your dad's?" Kathleen presses.

"Shut up." Lark tries to grab the diary from Kathleen, but Kathleen pulls it away. She turns to another drawing.

"Who are these people?" Kathleen asks.

"The Aluminum Ladies."

"They look like the Tin Man in *The Wizard of Oz*."

Lark says, "They're related."

Kathleen changes the subject. "Why do you have so many bottles?" Lark shrugs. "You have a lot. How long you been collecting them?"

Lark shrugs again. She picks up a red tequila bottle. "This was my first. Look at the horses standing up. They're carved right into the glass!"

Kathleen reads the label out loud. "*El Espiritu Del Agave.* Is that French?"

"Spanish. It means 'the spirit of the agave plant.' I asked Sister Jean."

"Is there really a spirit in there?" Kathleen asks, a little afraid. "Like in *I Dream of Jeannie*?"

"Yup. That's why they call alcohol 'spirits.'"

"No wonder you kept it. I couldn't throw away a bottle that

had a spirit in it." Kathleen picks up another bottle in Lark's collection and reads the label. "Bombay Sapphire."

"Isn't the glass the most peaceful lake color of blue?" Lark muses. "When I have a daughter, I'm going to name her Sapphire."

Kathleen examines the bottle. "Here's a picture of a queen."

Lark takes the bottle away. "Watch this. When I set it in front of the red spirit bottle, their light beams make purple." Lark sets the blue bottle on the window ledge in front of the red bottle, and sunbeams light up the glass and fall along the floor. She catches the purple beam in the palm of her hand. "Check me out: the wound of Jesus."

Scandalized, Kathleen slaps Lark's hand down. Lark turns away from Kathleen. Feeling bad about slapping Lark's hand, Kathleen picks up a Newcastle Ale bottle and reads its label. "The One and Only!" Lark takes that bottle from Kathleen, too, and puts it back away where it was.

"That's the 'me' bottle, 'The One and Only,'" Lark says. "Nobody has a life like mine."

"What makes you so special?"

"You don't wanna know."

"I know why you hang those bottles in the window. It's like a gargoyle on a church roof: to protect you from evil."

Lark mumbles, "I don't think it's working."

"Where'd you get all these bottles, anyway?" Kathleen asks.

"From Glassman."

"Lying is a sin."

Lark smiles like Mona Lisa and switches subjects. "You brought your Monkees album, didn't you?" Kathleen gives her the record. Lark puts it on.

"Davy is the cutest," Kathleen states the obvious.

"I always liked Michael because he's the smart one, and

nobody else likes him," Lark says.

"Yuck!" Kathleen grimaces.

"See?"

Scully opens the attic door.

"Daddy! You didn't knock."

"What are you doing that I'd have to knock for, huh?" Scully asks.

"We're not doing anything," Lark says. "Just listening to music."

Scully enters the room and picks up the Monkees record sleeve. "Long-haired hippie freaks." He takes the album off Lark's portable record player, scratching it in the process.

"Dad, no!"

"I don't want to be accused of exposing your little friend to subversive music. Those accusations can get out of hand."

"That's my record, Mr. Kurvas, not Lark's," Kathleen says timidly as she begins to gather her things. "I gotta go. Can you call my mom?"

Lark objects. "You said you were spending the night!"

"I changed my mind."

Scully hands Kathleen her record. "Nonsense. I was only kidding. Here's your record back."

Kathleen says, "I wanna go home."

Lark grabs her friend's arm. "You have to stay, Kathleen. We were gonna play Barbies. You brought yours."

"I brought Ken and Skipper too," Kathleen admits reluctantly.

"I have Barbie Cinderella," Lark counters.

"You do? Lemme see her."

Lark gets her Barbie storage case off the shelf. Kathleen goes to the other side of the room where her overnight gear is stored. She pulls out her Barbie carrying case. They compare every luxury option to determine whose case is better.

"Mine is lined with zebra skin. Pink and black," Lark says.

"Zebras aren't pink and black," Kathleen points out.

"Probably ate too many raspberries," Scully butts in. Both girls look at him with long-sufferance. "Okay, then. I'll leave you princesses to your Barbies. Catch you later."

21

A few hours later, the lights are off. The girls are asleep: Kathleen in Lark's bed and Lark on the floor in a blanket. As the attic door opens, a pale sliver of light falls across Lark's sleeping face.

The light beam widens to reveal all of Lark as the door is opening.

Scully climbs into the room. As he closes the door behind him, the beam of light on Lark slowly shrinks back down. Scully gets into Lark's bed, with Kathleen.

22

The next Monday in Lark's classroom, the fourth-grade girls sit at their desks in military rows with their hands folded. Almost no one is wiggling. Lark is at the chalkboard figuring out four digits divided by three digits in long division. Her teacher, Sister O'Day, smiles as she watches.

Lark gets the answer right. She turns to look at Kathleen for a thumbs-up. Instead, Kathleen quickly looks down at her paper, frowning. The school bell rings—recess time.

"All right, ladies. Line up!" the nun commands. The girls line up and walk from their classroom to the playground. Lark looks back at Kathleen, who is walking with Cindy.

When the line of girls arrives at the playground, they stand silently waiting for Sister O'Day to say they can go play. Lark looks back at Kathleen again.

"All right, girls. You may play." Joining girls of other grade levels on the asphalt playground, the fourth-graders shriek and run off in different directions: to the swings, to play jump rope or jacks, or to practice the hula hoop. Holding hands with Cindy, Kathleen runs away as Lark approaches her. Lark stands watching.

23

That afternoon, Lark lies on her bed with one knee up and the other leg crossed over it. She leans her journal up against her leg and writes another letter to Glassman.

Dear Glassman,
 I lost my only friend.
 My only other friend, I mean. You're my friend.
Sincerely yours,
Your friend,
Lark

She tears that page out of her journal and folds it like a paper airplane. Then something else occurs to her, and she unfolds the letter and adds a postscript.

P.S. I'd really like to see Glassland someday. Will you take me?

24

Three years later

Twelve years old now, Lark is moping around her backyard, kicking up fallen leaves, picking up stones and throwing them. She finds a baby bird among the leaves. She squats down to see it closer, then gets down on all fours so the baby bird can hear her. "You get kicked out too, little bird? That makes us sisters. C'mere." She scoops up the baby bird and looks at it closely. "I think you're going to be blue! Want me to put you back in your nest?"

Lark mouths a squeaky "Okay" like a ventriloquist, making the little bird talk. She carries it to Scully's man cave and speaks to him through the sheet.

"Daddy, the mommy bird kicked this baby bird out of the nest."

Scully opens the sheet and looks at the bird. "Maybe it just fell out."

"I can't reach high enough to put it back."

"Mother Bird will kick it out again for sure anyway. Once it's been manhandled, she won't take it back."

"But it isn't manhandled, Daddy. You forgot—I'm a bird."

"You're right. It's only been bird-handled. Still, I don't think its mother will allow it in the nest again."

"So can I keep it?"

"No." Scully waves at Lark to come into the man cave.

"I'll build a little nest, Daddy, and I'll bring worms, and I'll be a very nice mom."

"Imagine what your mother would say if she knew you had a creature in your room."

With a big wink at Scully, Lark says, "Maybe if I had a creature in my room, she'd be afraid to go in there!" They laugh conspiratorially.

"Scully?" Hattie yells, pulling the sheet aside. She sees Lark. "Oh, you're here too. What're you bothering your father for?"

"Nothing."

Scully pushes Lark behind him so Hattie won't see the bird. "She was just giving me a back rub." Lark quickly puts one hand on Scully's shoulder and begins kneading.

"Well, I'm going to church. I'm taking Rex with me. You're in charge of her."

"That'll be fine," Scully says.

Hattie walks away without saying goodbye. Scully calls after her. "I love you too!"

Scully drops the sheet back down and says to Lark, "That was close." They share a guilty smile, then Lark leaves the man cave and climbs the attic ladder.

Lark's bottle collection has grown. A beautiful chandelier made of bottles hangs from the light fixture. Melted globs of colored glass lie here and there.

The baby bird flops around on Lark's bedspread while Lark constructs a nest, weaving hair ribbons in and out the holes of a plastic strawberry basket, just the right size. Done with the weaving, Lark places the baby bird gently inside. "Okay. You stay right here. I'm going to get you some worms to eat. I should name you. I'll think of a good name while I'm hunting for worms."

Lark puts the nest on her dresser. She's on the way down the attic ladder when she meets Scully on his way up. He grabs hold of her foot.

"Kismet," he says.

Lark is focused on collecting worms. "What's that?"

"When two people run into each other at the perfect time."

"It's the perfect time for you to help me dig for worms." Lark tries to squeeze past Scully, who blocks her.

"Later. Go on back up." They both climb the ladder all the way. Once inside the attic, Scully lifts Lark and lays her on the bed.

"Not right now, Daddy."

"Yes, right now. It'll only take a minute."

"You always say that, and it always doesn't."

"This time it's gonna be different."

"No, Daddy. You're too heavy."

"It won't take long. Hold on."

"*Ow!* No, Daddy! That hurts! Stop!" Scully clasps his hand over her mouth.

"It only hurts the first time. I promise."

After Scully is finished, Lark says, "Daddy, I'm bleeding!"

"That's all right. You're supposed to bleed. You're a woman now."

In the strawberry basket, the little bird struggles for its life, then dies.

25

The next day, Lark comes out of the house wearing an outfit that's supposed to look like a priest's: Scully's long white shirt over her mom's long black skirt, and a construction-paper white cleric's collar. Rex is waiting at the bottom of the front steps of the house, with a red wagon full of flowers picked from neighbors' yards.

"What're you wearing?" Rex disapproves. "You can't be the priest."

"I'm the director. I can play whatever role I want."

"You don't have what it takes to be a priest."

"I do too!" Lark insists.

"I promise, you don't. Otherwise Mom would've named you John."

"What?"

"Only boys can be priests," Rex explains. "You have to be a man."

"No, you don't. That's silly."

"Oh yes you do! It's the law!"

"I'm gonna go ask Daddy."

"Go ahead."

Lark turns and walks back into the house. She heads for the garage, looking for Scully. Hattie sees her come in and calls her to the kitchen. Lark hesitates because of her costume, but she can't disobey.

Hattie ogles Lark up and down. "What are you supposed to be? Take off your dad's shirt right now. You'll have to iron that again. You've wrinkled it beyond hope."

Hattie makes Lark take off Scully's shirt right in front of her so that Lark stands there shirtless, humiliated, arms crossed in front of her breasts.

"You're too old to be playing costume." Hattie shoves the shirt back into Lark's hands. Lark clutches it to her chest. Hattie pulls it away again.

"Lemme see your breasts." Lark puts her arms down and lowers her head even more. "You need a bra. Is that my skirt you're wearing, you little thief?"

"I was gonna ask you, but you were on the phone, and I didn't think you'd mind."

"I mind." Hattie roughly pulls the skirt down. Lark steps hurriedly out of it. Now she's standing there in only her panties.

"I was gonna put it . . ."

Hattie interrupts. "I suppose you haven't started your woman flow yet, or you would've told me."

". . . back." Lark silently continues to stare at her mother's feet.

"Have you started?"

"Started what?"

"Your woman flow?"

"What's my woman flow?"

"Idiot. My Aunt Sally. Your period. Didn't they teach you this in school? Seems like there was a permission slip."

"Daddy wouldn't sign it."

"Then Daddy can darn well explain it to you. How old are you?"

"Gonna be . . ."

Hattie interrupts again. "A period's just like buying a new bag: once you got it, you don't want it anymore."

". . . thirteen."

Hattie walks away. She's finished with Lark.

A little while later, Lark comes out of the house again, this time dressed in her own long dress, with a huge doily draped over her head and shoulders like a mantilla. She bows to Rex. "You win. You be the priest. I'll play the grieving mother."

Rex solemnly pulls the wagon over to a tree where a small hole is already dug for the bird's grave. "Put it in the hole," he orders Lark. She sets the strawberry-basket nest in the hole first, then puts in a burrito made of wadded-up tin foil.

"Why'd you wrap it in tin foil?" Rex asks.

"So she wouldn't get dirty. Now say a prayer, Priest."

"Hail Mary, full of grace, the Lord is with thee. Blessed art thou amongst women, and blessed is the fruit of thy womb."

Lark pronounces the refrain. "Holy Mary, Mother of God, pray for us sinners, now and at the hour of our death."

"Baby bird wasn't a sinner. Birds don't sin; they're just birds."

"Crows steal," Rex says. Lark gives him that.

"What did you name the bird?" asks Rex.

"Sapphire."

"That's not a saint's name."

"She wasn't a Catholic."

26

Lark opens the door to the church confessional and goes in. It's a tiny, dark, wooden space with a kneeler and a small window. Lark kneels a few moments, then the window opens. Father Mulcahy speaks. "In the name of the Father, and of the Son, and of the Holy Ghost."

"Bless me, Father, for I have sinned."

"Please go ahead, Lark."

"I'll start with the easy ones. I dressed up like a priest. Is that a sin?"

"Did you perform any sacraments?"

"Only a funeral."

"That would be a sin," Father Mulcahy says.

"Mortal sin? Or venial?"

"Whose funeral?"

"A baby bird's. She wasn't Catholic."

"Venial sin," says the priest.

"Why can't I be a priest, anyway? I looked good in the collar."

"You're a young lady."

Lark argues, "I'll grow up."

"No, I mean young ladies don't grow up to be priests. They grow up to be wives and mothers."

"I don't want to be a wife and mother."

"Are you planning to be a nun?"

"Ha-ha. That's a good one, Father. But no. I'm gonna be a writer."

"Good luck with that. But going back to your sins, what else you got?"

Lark hesitates. "I've got this one sin I can't confess, because I swore I'd never tell anyone. Can you forgive me anyway?"

"No, I can't. Confess your sin to me, as an emissary of God, and I'll talk to God about forgiving you."

"Can't you forgive me for a secret sin?"

"It's not a secret to God. He already knows what you've done."

"Oh, good! Then I don't have to tell you. Problem solved." Lark stands up and opens the confessional door.

"That's not exactly how it works," Father Mulcahy tries to say, but Lark talks over him.

"Ten Hail Marys, like usual?"

"Better add in a novena to the Blessed Virgin, to atone for your secret sin."

"You got it, Father."

27

Beside the loose board in the back fence, Lark finds a purple bag with gold stitching. It says "Crown Royal." Inside, Lark finds a cut-glass decanter with a purple-and-gold label. "No note," she says out loud. She bravely peeks her head out through the hole in the fence. No Glassman. She'd been hoping to see him this time. She pulls a little reporter's notepad out of her blouse pocket and writes Glassman a letter.

Dear Glassman,
   Thank you for the purple bag.
   I like the bottle a lot also.
   Can I write a story about you?
   I'm starting a newspaper at school.
   I'm calling it The Fluke, *because I got that word wrong on a spelling bee, and I didn't know what it meant, so I looked it up. It means something that happens by chance. I think it's a good name.*
   Please write me back and tell me when we can meet so I can interview you.
Your friend,
Lark

A few days later, Lark finds a note and a dark-blue liquor bottle at the loose board.

I think it's best that we remain secret friends.
Glassman

28

Happily, Lark hums Chopin as she enters the living room. Her mood drops slightly when she sees Hattie, but then she brightens again. She has news. "*Um . . .*"

"In the name of Saint Pete, what do you want?" Hattie is measuring for curtains. She puts Lark to work. "Here, hold the end of this." She hands Lark the end of the measuring tape.

"*Um . . .* I won a writing contest. At school. They gave me this book."

Hattie says, "Put it down and stand over there."

Lark reluctantly sets down *The Rhyming Dictionary.* Hattie points for her to stand at the edge of the window. Lark accidentally lets go of the measuring tape, and *zip-zap*, it rewinds itself back up and hits Hattie.

"You did that on purpose!" she screams.

"I didn't. I swear to God."

"Get out of here, you ungrateful you-know-what."

Lark is stunned silent, then angry.

"Maybe God'll give me cancer so I can just die. Just plain die." She grabs her new book and runs out and climbs her attic stairs. At her desk, Lark writes another letter.

Dear Glassman,
  Today I won a writing contest.
  First place.
  They gave me a rhyming dictionary,
  so I wrote you a poem about glass:
    "At last, the vast glass mass flashed past."
  Not a very good poem, but it rhymes.
Lark

29

Along the sidewalk, up the Catholic church steps, and through the doors winds a line of preteens in green choir robes, the girls all wearing a variety of chapel veils on their heads. Each kid is paired with an adult of the same sex. Lark is paired with Georgia. Kathleen and her sponsor walk just ahead of Lark and Georgia.

Lark suddenly pats the top of her own head. "I forgot my chapel veil!"

"*No problemo.*" Georgia pulls a Kleenex out of her purse, then keeps looking until she finds a bobby pin. She pins the little tissue to Lark's hair. "A Girl Scout is always resourceful. 'Course your mother won't be pleased if it shows in the pictures."

"Look!" Lark whispers. "Here comes the bishop. Check out his outfit."

Georgia approves. "The shepherd's crook is a nice touch."

As the bishop enters the church, he hands his staff and miter to one of his two attendant altar boys.

A railing with a kneeler runs all the way along in front of the altar and down the sides, a low fence to keep laymen out of sacred space. The candidates for confirmation process down the aisle to the tune of *O Sacrum Convivium*, then kneel at the railing with their sponsors standing behind them. The bishop sits in the red velvet chair that Father Mulcahy sits in during silent prayer.

Father Mulcahy is preparing oils and holy water, hanging a linen towel over his arm like a maître d'.

The ceremony begins. The bishop rises, dons his miter, and picks up his staff, and then takes center stage in the altar enclosure. He holds one hand over his brow and squints, as if focusing his sights on a clay bird before firing. From among the boys on the north side of the altar, he hones in on the class clown and points at him. "Do you believe in God, the Father Almighty, Creator of heaven and earth?"

The class clown channels the Cowardly Lion, "I do, I do, I do believe."

A titter whispers through the church. The bishop ignores it, pointing at a girl. "Do you believe in Jesus Christ, who was born of the Virgin Mary, crucified, and buried?"

"I do," she answers.

Cindy, kneeling on the other side of Kathleen, whispers to Lark, "Nice chapel veil." Kathleen giggles. The bishop eyes the row of tweens, trying to identify the source of the sound. He picks Lark.

"Do you renounce Satan?"

Lark faints. She bumps her head on the guardrail as she slumps down. Georgia eases her to the floor.

30

Moments later in the sacristy—the tiny room behind the altar—Lark sits with her head between her legs in another massive red-velvet chair. Georgia bends over her. "Good job not drawing attention to yourself. Did you eat anything this morning?"

"No. You're supposed to fast before the sacrament."

"Dumb rule," Georgia says. "I never follow it."

"You don't?"

"It's not a mortal sin, so I risk it. Ha!" Lark is appalled and titillated. "Boy, I'm a super godmother, aren't I? I'm supposed to set a good example."

"I always thought Jesus could tell if you have food in your stomach, because when you swallow the host, he gets in there and he can see it. That's how he knows."

"God's usually not paying attention to our little old tummies," Georgia says. "Too busy with ball teams."

The confirmation ceremony concludes, and the bishop enters the sacristy. "Where's the little patient?"

Lark raises her hand. "I'm sorry I wrecked your sacrament."

"No, no, no. All things are good in God's plan."

"Maybe God wanted you to meet the bishop personally," Georgia suggests. Lark sits up to show respect for the bishop, but she gets dizzy again, and puts her head back between her legs.

The bishop says, "That must be it! Kismet." Lark peers up at him suspiciously. He asks, "What saint did you choose to be your patron saint?"

"It's a secret," says Lark.

"God knows all secrets, and I'm the emissary of God, so tell me."

"Dymphna."

"Dymphna," repeats the Bishop.

"Yes."

"And why did you choose Dymphna?" he asks.

"*Um* . . . I kind of liked how it sounds, like a nymph," Lark tries.

Georgia scolds her, "That's no reason to pick a saint."

"What do you know about Dymphna?" the bishop asks.

"Her father cut her head off."

"Lots of people got their heads cut off. That's not enough to be sainted. What else did she do?"

"Well, she ran away with a priest," Lark says.

"Be serious," Georgia admonishes.

"I'm not making this up. I read it in a book."

"Why did she run away?" The bishop encourages her.

"Because she didn't want to marry her father." Lark speaks fast. "Her mother died, so her father wanted to marry Dymphna, but she said, 'No,' and ran away with the priest, so her father cut off her head."

The bishop tells Georgia, "Leave us."

"Your Grace." Georgia wiggles her finger goodbye at Lark, who returns the gesture. When Georgia is clear of the room, the bishop leans kindly toward Lark and asks, "Is this happening to you?"

"What, Your Highness?"

"Is your father wanting you to be his wife?"

Behind her back, Lark crosses the fingers of her left hand, which makes it okay to lie. Playground rules.

"No, Your Highness."

"You can tell me," he says.

"Cross my heart and hope to die," she says, crossing her heart with the hand that isn't crossing fingers, knowing that probably damned her.

"Why did you choose Dymphna?"

"It was my mother's confirmation name. She gave it to me with this holy medal." She holds it up for him to see.

That seemed to satisfy him. "All right then. Let's get you confirmed." With his thumb, the bishop makes the Sign of the Cross on Lark's forehead. "Dymphna, be sealed with the Gift of the Holy Spirit."

Lark sits there silently. The bishop waits for her to speak. She doesn't know what to say.

"Thank you?"

He smiles. "How about amen?"

"Oh yeah. Amen."

"That's it. You're confirmed," the bishop finishes.

"That was it? I'm confirmed? But I wasn't even kneeling."

"I think God will overlook it this time."

31

Lit by her Cinderella carriage night light, Lark lies in her bed under the covers. She hears Scully climbing her ladder. She rolls over on her stomach and pretends to be asleep.

Scully comes in and closes the trap door behind him. He sits on the edge of Lark's bed and begins rubbing her back. "Hey there, Oriole! Wake up, wake up, sleepyhead!"

Lark pretends not to hear.

Scully sings, "Wake up, wake up! The birds are singing. Cock-a-doodle-doo!" Scully lies down beside Lark, scooting her over. She rolls away and stands up on the other side of the bed.

"No, Daddy."

"Too tired for a snuggle? Come on, I'll be quick."

"No. The bishop erased all my sins. I don't want to get any new ones on my soul."

"Love is never a sin."

"It's a sin."

"Who told you that?"

"I just know."

Scully gets out of the bed. "It's those damn nuns, isn't it? I never wanted you to go to that school."

"It's not the nuns. It's me."

"I know what this is," Scully says. "You're getting your period!

You're turning into a witch! It's natural. I've been expecting it."

"I haven't had any period yet."

"Well, judging by your mood, you're due for one soon. I'll give you your space, then, Kiwi."

"Thank you, Daddy."

"De nada."

32

As Lark's fellow seventh-grade girls file out of their grammar school classroom, Lark hands each of them a mimeographed newsletter, *The Fluke*. At the end of the file of girls comes Sister Columba. Lark hands her a newsletter too. Walking away, Sister Columba looks at the headline.

Was Lot a Righteous Man?

She quietly reads aloud.

Lot was the only good one in Sodom and Gomorrah, which is why God burned down the cities. His wife turned into salt because she looked back.

Lot's daughters didn't have any names. They went to live in a cave with their dad because the city was gone and there was no place else to live.

Sister Columba likes it so far. "Missed a comma, but nice writing, Lark. You must have a talented English teacher. Oh yeah, that would be me!" Sister Columba curtsies and continues reading.

Then Lot's daughters got pregnant. The Bible says it was their fault that their dad got drunk. I think it was their father's fault! What do you think? Write a Letter to the Editor.

Lark points at her own name in print. "That's me," she beams. "I'm the editor."

Sister Columba asks, "Where did you do your research?"

"I read the book of Lot's daughters in the school library."

"And what did the book tell you?"

"That it was the daughters' fault."

"And what does the Bible say?"

"That it was the daughters' fault."

"And you question the Bible?"

"No, Sister, swear to God. But I still think it was their father's fault."

"Lark!" Sister Columba snaps, but Lark doesn't stop.

"He probably got himself drunk."

Sister Columba takes Lark by the shoulder, roughly. "You're going straight to the principal's office, young lady."

"But it makes sense," Lark insists.

"Lot was a righteous man," says Sister Columba with finality. "His daughters were damned for what they did."

"I know."

33

"Expelled!" Hattie yells. "I've never been more embarrassed! Now what am I supposed to do with you until summer camp starts?"

"Send me to the pagan babies."

Hattie and Lark have just arrived home from Lark's school. Lark heads straight up to her attic room. Hattie follows behind, up the ladder, a brave act for somebody with an enemy's foot at head-level. Hattie risks it because she doesn't want to miss Lark's reaction when she sees Lark's glass window curtain dashed to bits. Broken bottlenecks still hang, sharp as dragon's teeth, gothic. The floor is covered with glass shards.

"You clean up this mess before somebody gets hurt." Once Hattie's head has retreated from the trapdoor hole, Lark mimes kicking the ladder down, but she doesn't really do it. She looks under her bed. Hattie hadn't found her hidden bottles under there. These are the special bottles: the ones that still have booze in them. Lark chooses a bottle of brandy and takes a swig. She sinks down to the carpet, the shattered glass pressing against her legs. She takes another swig.

Sitting at her desk with the bottle of brandy, Lark stares at the headless corpse of the broken turkey bottle as she composes another letter to Glassman.

Dear Glassman,
  I want to go to Glassland.
  Please kidnap me.
Lark

Lark tucks the letter into an envelope and sprinkles broken glass inside. She carefully licks the flap and closes the envelope.

34

Later, standing in the hallway outside the bathroom door, Scully hears Lark retching. Without knocking, he opens the door and goes in. Lark is standing over the toilet, gagging.

"What's wrong, Blue Jay?" Scully asks kindly.

"I'm dying," Lark tells him.

"You're not dying."

"I'm dying, and I'm going to hell."

Scully puts his hands on Lark's shoulders. "You're not going to hell."

"Yes, I am. Yes, we are. It's wrong, Daddy, what we do. So I'm going to hell, and you are too."

"Nonsense. Just say a few prayers."

"That's what Father told me."

Scully's eyes squint. "Father Mulcahy?" Lark tells him yes. Fearing that Lark has given him up to his old friend, Scully bites his lip. "What did you tell him?" Lark remains silent. "What did he say?"

"Ten Hail Marys."

Scully laughs. "And did you say them?"

"No."

"That's all that's wrong with you, then. You need a little forgiveness."

"Does that make you throw up?" Lark asks. "Not saying your penance?"

"You've been throwing up? Sometimes that goes along with getting your period."

"I haven't got any period yet."

"You will soon. Look how your breasts have grown." He grabs one of Lark's breasts.

"Ouch! That hurts!"

"It does? Sorry. Come on out of the bathroom. I'll get you some Pepto Bismol."

"I can't," Lark says. "I've got to wash my hands."

"Then wash them."

She turns on the faucet and soaps her hands. She spends a long time sudsing them up. She rubs each finger separately and lathers her wrists and arms.

"For goodness sakes, Hummingbird! It's not like you've been gardening."

"I'm saying the ABCs to myself. That's how long you're supposed to wash."

"XYZ . . . Now come with me," Scully says.

Lark rinses one finger at a time. Finally, she turns off the faucet and dries her hands.

"Geez," Scully mutters. "Okay, they're dry, let's go!"

Lark heads for the door and touches the doorknob, drawing back her hand as if it were hot. She stands frozen with her hand in the air. Her dad pushes her aside and opens the bathroom door. "Come on."

Lark doesn't follow him. She stands like a statue. He reaches into the bathroom to draw her out, but she backs away.

"I can't. The doorknob has germs." She does an about-face back to the sink and turns on the faucet. Again, she lathers her hands.

"Are you crazy? You just did that." Scully reenters the bathroom and grabs Lark's elbow. She shrugs him off.

"I'm dirty," she says. "I have to wash."

"I don't under—"

"Leave me alone!"

"All right, Mockingbird. Wash yourself all you want. Just don't use up all the soap."

35

The bell rings as Scully enters a tiny *botanica* stuffed with statues of Catholic saints and Hindu goddesses, incense, souvenirs, and canned beverages. Doña Paloma, the proprietress from El Salvador, wearing colorful scarves and flowing robes, greets Scully.

"Ah, I see you're back again. How did it work, that tea I sold you last time?" Doña Paloma mimes carrying a huge penis in front of her. Scully drags Lark out from behind himself and poses her in front of him like a human shield. Doña Paloma quits fooling around, wipes her hands on her apron, and pinches Lark on the cheek and then the shoulder.

"Too skinny," she concludes.

"Doña, no. She's my daughter!"

Doña Paloma is perturbed. "Then what're you here for?" Scully hems and haws and points at Lark.

"I haven't got my period yet," Lark says.

"How old are you, child?"

"Gonna be thirteen."

"When you gonna be?"

"Next year."

"And how long since your last period?"

"I never had a period."

"Then how do you know it's late?"

"Daddy said."

Scully stares at his shoes.

"She's in no hurry to be a woman," Doña Paloma concludes. To Lark she says, "Go home. Stay away from boys. Your dragon's blood will be on you soon enough."

"But, Doña, please," Scully begs. "If you check the girl, perhaps you'll find the blockage."

Doña Paloma pulls Lark behind the curtain that separates the front of the store from her little office. "So tell me about your boyfriend."

"I don't have a boyfriend."

"I'm just going to feel your tummy. Be still." Lark giggles.

Moments later, Doña Paloma tears the curtain as she throws it open. Behind her, Lark smooths down her skirt.

"May you rot in purgatory twelve times twelve lifetimes before Lucifer drags you to hell," Doña Paloma whispers furiously.

Scully whispers back. "I know."

"I can't help you. Take her to an abortionist."

"We can't have an abortion. We're Catholic."

With a key from her massive ring, Paloma unlocks a small brass safe and takes out a glass jar of loose tea. In a little white paper bag, she mixes a scoop of the special tea with a pinch of this and that. From the office, Lark asks, "Can I come out now?"

Doña Paloma puts on a public face. "Of course you can, *Mommi.*"

"Why are you calling me *mommi*?"

"It's a Salvadoran thing. It means 'little girl.' And I know how much little girls like tea parties." Lark nods sheepishly. Doña Paloma gives her the package of tea. "Now have a cup of this tea when you get home. You will soon begin bleeding.

Don't worry about this. Bleeding is what women are supposed to do."

"I know. Daddy told me that."

Doña Paloma takes Lark by the shoulders. "You ever need any help, I am your sister. You understand? You can always come to me. My name is Paloma."

"Paloma. Sounds like music. I'm Lark."

"Paloma is a bird name, just like Lark. It means 'dove.' See! We really are sisters! Good luck to you, Sister Bird. My phone number's in the bag. If anything goes wrong, call me first." Lark cuddles the bag of tea to her chest and turns to walk away.

"Thank you, Sister Paloma." She smiles at her dad and says, "I have a sister."

36

Back in Lark's bedroom, she is sitting at her desk swallowing the last of her tea. Scully stands behind her, petting her back. "Now then, where did I leave off tickling you last time?"

Lark suddenly lets out a gasp of pain.

"What is it?" Scully asks.

"I'm dying."

"You're not dying. Let's see." He lifts her skirt.

"Daddy!" she protests, swatting his hand away.

But he has seen blood on her underwear. "Looks like a period, all right. Better go on into the bathroom and fix yourself up." Scully gives Lark a box of sanitary napkins with an elastic belt. "I think the directions are written in there somewhere." Lark takes the box, unsure of herself. "You'll be all right, Seagull. It's very normal."

Lark climbs down the ladder to the bathroom. She stands at the sink reading the directions on the sanitary napkin box and playing cat's cradle with the belt that came in the package. Suddenly she doubles over with another pain. "Help me, Christopher Robin!" she pants. Overwhelmed by another sharp contraction, she pushes with all her might while grunting a long grunt. The pain stops. Something has passed.

Lark reaches into her underwear and takes something out.

She freezes with wonder. She wraps it in a washcloth and is holding it the way little girls hold baby dolls, when Scully opens the door and walks into the bathroom. Lark shows him the washcloth excitedly. "Look what came with my period!"

Even though Scully knew this would happen, he isn't prepared to look at what's in the washcloth. He stutters. "That's . . . that's normal. That's how periods start. That's what always happens."

"What is it?" Lark asks.

Scully tries to take it away from Lark to flush it down the toilet. "It's just a practice baby. You get one with your first period. Didn't your mother tell you about that?"

"No."

"Give it to me." He flushes the toilet and tries again to take the washcloth from Lark.

"No!" screams Lark. "It'll drown!"

"Silly. It's not alive."

Lark backs away. Scully follows her. Lark argues desperately. "And it'll clog up your plumbing, the way I clogged it that time. You were really mad. Remember?"

Scully laughs. "Wasn't funny at the time. Now, give it to me."

Lark pleads, "Can't I keep it?"

"You're a crazy little birdie," Scully shakes his head. "You can't keep dead things."

"It's not dead."

Scully kneels down so he's more at Lark's eye-level. "Honey . . . it's . . ." He lifts the corner of the washcloth and bellows, "Not dead!"

"Shush, Daddy, you scared it."

"Quick! Lemme baptize her! Otherwise she'll go to limbo! Give her to me."

"No."

"Then hold her over the sink. I'll have to be the priest since no one else is here." Lark jealously holds on to the washcloth. Scully soothes her. "It only takes a few drops of water." He runs his fingers under the sink faucet to wet them. Lark backs into the corner trying to protect her bundle, to keep it away from Scully, but Scully waves his wet hand and sprinkles a few drops of water into the air and onto Lark and the washcloth.

"In the name of the Father, Son, and Holy Ghost, I baptize thee, *um* . . . what name shall we call her?"

"Sapphire," says Lark with assurance.

"Sapphire?" Scully repeats.

"Sapphire the Second. That's her name."

"I don't know that there's a saint name in there, but then I don't know that there isn't. I baptize thee, Sapphire, in the name of the Father, the Son, and the Holy Ghost. As it was in the beginning, is now, and ever shall be, world without end."

Sapphire stops wiggling. Lark beams. "It's a miracle! She stopped wiggling right when you did that!"

"Lark, honey, give it to me."

"No, We're good."

"But you need to . . ."

Lark speaks through her teeth. "Not. Right. Now." She pushes past Scully and out the door, then climbs the ladder to her attic bedroom, carefully cradling Sapphire in one hand. She places her pillow in the center of her bed and lays the washcloth on it. She uses the edges of the washcloth to wipe blood off Sapphire.

Next, she takes out her case of Barbie clothes and chooses a little pink party dress with little pink Barbie shoes. "Too big," she says. She looks around the room and spots her toy angel wearing a golden robe just the right size for Sapphire. Lark takes it down from the shelf and removes its clothing.

Scully pushes up the trap door to the attic and finds Lark, Sapphire, and the naked angel on the bed. Lark doesn't seem to notice Scully as she puts the golden robe on Sapphire. "If I wish hard enough, I can get you out of limbo," she whispers.

"No limbo. She's baptized. Straight to heaven, Birdie," Scully says. "She's your guardian angel now."

"She looks like an angel. See, I put my angel's robe on her."

"I told Hattie you'd skip dinner because you weren't feeling well."

"Sort of not a lie."

Lark reclines on the bed and cuddles Sapphire's pillow. Scully stands over her with empty hands raised.

"Now, Birdie look at me. Practice babies never survive." Scully takes hold of Lark's chin and makes her look at him. "Sapphire is dead."

"How do you know she's dead unless you killed her?"

"Listen. She's not breathing. Her heart's not beating."

Lark carefully lays her ear against Sapphire. "You killed her with your holy water."

"It wasn't holy water, it was sink water, not even blessed."

"Then the baptism didn't work, did it?"

"Yes, it did. Jesus makes exceptions."

Lark cheers up a little. "We'll have to have a funeral."

Scully says, "For sure."

"We can bury her next to Sapphire the First."

"You buried a sapphire?"

Exasperated, Lark reminds him, "That was the bird's name—remember the little bird? I found it and it died, remember? That day . . ."

He interrupts. "I do recall that event."

Lark walks over to her dresser and picks up a pretty jewelry box. "This'll work." She dumps trinkets and costume jewelry out, then lays the jewelry box on the bed. Gingerly, she nestles Sapphire into her tiny crypt.

Scully stands by, helpless. "Look, Tweetie Bird, I know I don't say it as much as I should, but I love you. More than anyone else on earth will ever love you."

Lark looks at him with hatred. He sees the look and is shocked at its depth.

"And I want you to sing 'Amazing Grace,'" Lark directs him.

"What time? The funeral, I mean?"

"Sunset. Leave us alone now."

37

Scully retrieves a bottle of bourbon from the kitchen counter and carries it to the bathroom. He leans against the sink and drinks out of the bottle, then sets the bottle on the floor. He gets to work cleaning up drops of blood, then he gingerly picks up the bloody bathmat and carries it outside.

He opens the alley gate, holding the bathmat. A man stands beside the tailgate of a small pickup truck with glass bottles piled up in its bed.

"Kitty gave birth on the rug," Scully says. The man nods and doffs his hat. He gets into his pickup truck and drives to the next set of trash cans.

At sunset, underneath the maple tree, two little graves lie decorated with bits of colored glass. Scully and Lark kneel beside them. "Pray for us sinners, now and at the hour of our death." They rise to their feet and dust their knees.

"Now, Daddy," Lark directs.

Scully begins to sing. "Amazing grace, how sweet the sound that saved a wretch like me." But he chokes up and can't finish.

38

A few days later, Lark is hanging out beside the graves, quietly singing. She hears a truck door slam in the alley behind her house, and she gets up and runs to the gate.

Nothing scares her now.

She steps out into the alley. "Glassman?" she asks the man standing there.

"Glassman?" the man asks back.

"Take me to Glassland."

"Glassland?"

"Please. You have to take me."

"I do?"

A pickup truck piled high with glass bottles is parked behind Lark's gate. Lark climbs up into the bed of the truck and settles amid the bottles. "I'll ride back here."

Lark's neighbor to the north opens his own gate and carries brown paper bags of trash into the alley. He sees Lark in the back of the truck, then notices a man standing there. "Hey, what are you doing with that little girl in your truck?"

Lark tries to stand up in the back of the truck, saying, "It's okay." But she slips, and a broken bottle splits open her hand. She bites her lips and doesn't scream. It's bleeding a lot. "Hurry Glassman! C'mon, let's go!"

Another neighbor comes out to the alley. "What's happening, man?"

Lark scoops her hand in the air, shooing Glassman toward her. But he doesn't drive off a hundred miles an hour and leave the neighbors behind. He doesn't even get into the truck. "Go on, get out," he says to Lark.

Hattie wobbles out of the gate. "He's an Alley Man! They steal little girls. I've always told her so." She screams back through the gate, "Scully! Get out here! Hurry!"

Hattie shakes her fist at Lark. "Don't say I didn't warn ya!" Hattie realizes she is being watched, and switches into good mother mode. "My baby!" she fake cries. "Someone help!"

"No! No help!" Lark says. "He's my friend!"

Scully crashes through the gate, a little drunk, gun drawn. "What's going on?" The man beside the truck puts his hands up. Scully sees the bloody Lark in the back of the truck. Scully aims his gun. Lark leans out of the truck as far as she can to stop the bullet, but to no avail.

Scully shoots the man, who falls to the ground. Scully drops the gun and hurries to Lark. Stepping over the body, he lifts her out of the truck. A neighbor crouches beside the dead man, checking for a pulse.

Hattie sidles up to another neighbor and puts her hand on his shoulder flirtatiously. "I told her a thousand times if I told her once, stay away from Alley People."

Scully holds Lark in his arms. As she stares down at the bloody corpse, Scully pets her hair. "You're safe now, Robin. Daddy's got you."

39

Fifty years later

In a hoarder's cluttered studio apartment, Lark, now in her sixties, nests in her unmade bed typing on her laptop, surrounded by stuffed animals, books, clean and unclean clothes, and a dish or two. She's wearing mismatched pajamas and a tiara, and her silver Saint Dymphna medal on a chain. Her hands are chapped, her nails bitten.

She stops typing to read the last lines she's been writing.

Scully holds Lark in his arms as she stares down at the bloody corpse. Scully pets her hair, saying, "You're safe now, Birdie. Daddy's got you."

Lark's cell phone rings. She closes her laptop and puts it on top of the pile on her bed, then digs among the toys and pillows, tossing them aside as she goes. She pulls her still-ringing cell phone out and looks at it. "Unknown." She tucks the phone under a stuffed elephant.

Now she can't find her laptop. She stands up and balances in bare feet on the mattress. Channeling Harpo Marx, she heaves Beanie Babies and paperbacks off the bed, looking. Her cell phone slips to the floor. She finds the laptop and pulls it out of the pile, but the power cord has wrapped itself around her ankle. As she disentangles that, the phone rings again. It stops ringing, then rings again at once. It rings a few more times, then stops. Immediately, it begins to ring again. "All right already. I give in," Lark says. She hunts for the phone, throwing socks into the air as she searches. Finally, she steps down off the mattress and onto the phone. It stops ringing. "Well, that's one way."

She picks up the phone and examines the screen. It rings in her hand. She answers. "What's so important? Hello? Hello?" The caller has hung up. "Well, diddly do," she says to no one, "I was finished anyway. The End. I forgot to write The End. Oh well, maybe it's not really the end yet." She looks at her phone. "Time for my phone meeting."

Lark pushes clothing out of the way and squeezes into her overflowing closet. In the corner of the closet is a somewhat open space with a beanbag chair and a teddy bear. She sits down and closes the closet door almost all the way. Illuminated by the light of her cell phone, she dials a number. She hears the tones of the numbers pushed, then the recorded voice, "You will now be placed into the conference. There are currently seven other participants in the conference." She hunkers down and sighs.

Malea is on the phone. Like the inside of a gypsy wagon, Malea's walls are hung with scarves and necklaces and oil paintings and photographs. Tchotchkes cover every surface of her shabby antique furniture. Malea is wearing a floor-length caftan with a gold lamé turban, heavy makeup, and dangling earrings. She speaks with a Creole accent, in a falsetto. Malea is a transgendered woman. "Welcome to a telephone meeting of Victims of Incest," she says.

Other phone callers say in unison, "We are not to blame, and we are not alone."

Malea continues, "Welcome, everybody. Let's see who's here on the phone call this beautiful day—or night, depending on where you are on earth. We'll go around the virtual room and introduce ourselves by saying our first names and where we're calling from. I'll start. I'm Malea in New Orleans."

"Hi, Malea," the callers all say.

Fergie, a tiny Filipino in his thirties, sits on a low wall in front of the Bellagio on the Las Vegas Strip. The fountains play behind him. "Howdy, everybody, I'm Fergie, calling from Nevada."

"Hi, Fergie," everyone says.

Pippi's apartment looks theatrical. Photographs of Pippi herself in different costumes decorate the walls: she's a famous actress. Over a view of Times Square with its gigantic movie screens, red velvet curtains drape her windows as if they were hanging in front of a stage. Gowns spill out of her many suitcases. Martha, Pippi's personal assistant, is hanging dresses up on hangers and carrying them into the bedroom. Pippi dramatically collapses on a purple chaise lounge.

"Hi, everybody. Whew! Practically didn't make it. This is Pippi. Where am I? Lemme look. I'm in Manhattan. Am I glad to be here! In the meeting, I mean, not in Manhattan, although it is great to be tripping the light fantastic here on 42nd Street. I pass."

"Hi, Pippi," the phone callers say.

From her closet, Lark speaks into the phone. "Hi, I'm Lark in Los Angeles."

Everyone says, "Hi, Lark."

Verena, a plump blonde, pulls yellow leaves from her rose bushes and cuts off dead blooms with a clippers. "This is Verena in Switzerland."

"Hi, Verena."

Amitza is using Skype to call in to the meeting. Her

state-of-the-art technology and modern room decor contrast with the full burka and veil she's wearing. "Amitza here. I'm in Egypt."

"Hi, Amitza." After a few moments Malea says, "Welcome, everybody."

Klevon interrupts. "Klevon in Quebec."

"Welcome, Klevon," Malea says. "Who else wants to say hi?"

Louise rocks in a wicker chair on her back porch and knits as she listens to the meeting on speaker. She suddenly realizes she should announce herself. She nervously drops her knitting and picks up the speaker and talks into it. "Hi. Louise in Oregon."

Malea says, "Welcome, Louise. Welcome, everybody. This meeting is for adult women and men who were victimized as children by the crime of childhood incest. Who will read the Introduction to the Meeting?"[1]

"Oh, I will! I will!" shouts Pippi.

"Thank you, Pippi," Malea says.

Pippi pats her chaise lounge, looking for the script. She picks up a script, but it's the wrong one. She gets up from the couch and leafs through a decorous fan of scripts on the coffee table. "I can't find the script, but I know it by heart. Okay. Let's see. Incest is taboo in most societies, yet it occurs in all. The taboo seems not to be committing incest but talking about it. In meetings, we break this silence. We have no more secrets."

Everyone chimes in, "We will speak, we will be heard, and we will heal."

Pippi's assistant, Martha, finds the meeting script and hands it to Pippi. "Oh, here's the script." She continues reading. "Incest victims may be male, female, gay, lesbian, transgendered, asexual, or queer. Rich and poor, the elite to the ordinary, all nationalities, all races, and all religions, or none."

Klevon responds to the reading by mouthing the words. Pippi

continues. "We victims of childhood incest have many things in common, like compulsive behaviors such as alcoholism, drug addiction, overeating, anorexia, overspending, gambling, sex addiction, and workaholism."

Louise nods her head in agreement, then sees a mistake in her knitting and tears it out. Pippi reads on. "Some of us may bite our nails, pick at our cuticles, cut or burn ourselves, or pull out our hair. Our minds use these mechanisms to help us block out the horror."

She finishes up with pathos. "When we try to have relationships, they are usually as abusive as our childhoods were. Some of our fellows have committed suicide. We struggle on a daily basis just to be okay." Pippi puts down the script. "That's all of it. I pass, Malea."

"Pippi, thank you for reading," Malea says. "If you identify with what's been read, you're in the right place. And now we'll begin the sharing. Who would like to share first?"

"Klevon in Quebec. I'd like to share."

"Please go ahead, Klevon."

Klevon is a black Canadian, about forty years old, and sickly. He lies in bed beneath a Native American blanket in his small apartment, which is decorated with other Native American collectibles: baskets, a feathered headdress, and a beaded shirt hang on the wall. "I'm sick today. I'm sick almost every day. I have the incest disease, fibromyalgia. I call it the incest disease because I hear so many other people on this phone line saying they have it too. Stuffing down shameful secrets causes this illness. I don't want to be sick, but some things have to stay secrets in the real world, don't they? The real world can't handle some secrets. Have to be hushed up."

Klevon reaches painfully for a glass of water on the table beside his bed. He sucks through the straw, then puts the glass down. As he lies back in bed, he starts to choke on the water. He coughs for a few moments, then regains his composure.

"How could I ever tell people about this? 'Nice to meet you. Who, me? Why, I'm an incest survivor. No, I don't work. No, I don't go to school. I just survive.' I could never say that to anyone—anyone but you folks on the phone line."

Hunched over the cell phone he clutches to his ear as if it's a lifeline, Fergie jumps off the Bellagio wall and bumps into a pedestrian walking in the other direction. He accidentally unmutes his phone, interrupting Klevon. "Oh, sorry! I'm sorry. I didn't mean . . ."

"Is that you, Fergie?" Klevon asks. "Please mute your phone."

"Oh, sorry! I'm really, really sorry, Klevon. Forgive me. I was listening. I must've accidentally hit the unmute button. I'm sorry!"

"No worries, Fergie. Happens to the best of us," Malea says. "Please go ahead, Klevon."

"I wanted to say that I don't have any friends except you folks on the phone. How can anyone be my friend if they don't know about the incest? There'll always be a giant hole in the relationship if I don't tell them. But when I've told people about it before, they've disappeared from my life. Good friends, best friends, they couldn't handle it. *Poof*, they're outta there. No, I can't tell regular people. But in here, on the phone line, I can say it. I'm an incest survivor. I like the survivor part. Thank you. I pass."

"Thank you, Klevon," Malea says. "Who's next?"

"I'll be next," Verena pipes up. As she shares, Verena dumps her basket of dead blooms into the trash. She takes off her gloves. "So I'm Verena, and I have something to say that's happy. Today I went to a yoga class. I actually left the house!" The other phone callers clap for Verena.

"I know, it's huge. And I spent an hour with people, which I'd usually avoid like a colonoscopy. I have you all to thank. You on the phone line. You're teaching me that I'm not alone. One out of four children is molested, so I'm definitely not alone. I pass."

On Lark's phone, another phone call beeps in. "Diddly." Lark mutes the incest support meeting and switches over to the other call. "Hello?"

"Lark! What a delight to hear your voice."

"Says who?"

"Georgia O'Donnell, your mom's best friend." Georgia is calling from Hattie and Scully's home as it is today: decorated with items from the '70s and '80s, the last decades they brought things into the house. Scully, now in his eighties, lies on a rented hospital bed in the middle of their living room with Hattie hovering over him. Georgia is on the phone to Lark from the kitchen table, trying to be inconspicuous so Hattie doesn't notice.

"Mrs. O'Donnell? I remember you," Lark says. "You're like my godmother or something."

"I've been derelict in my duties," Georgia admits.

"Yeah, I've gone all to hell."

Georgia looks around at Scully and Hattie. Hattie is fussing with Scully's blankets, holding up his catheter bag to the light, compulsively rearranging the items on his hospital tray table. "It's about your dad."

Lark climbs out of the closet. "We're estranged."

"I know that, Lark, but he's dying."

"So?"

"Your mother wants you to come."

Lark harrumphs. "She does not. She wants Rex to come, not me."

"All right, then, I want you to come. Bury the hatchet."

"In his head," Lark mumbles.

"The hospice nurse told me to call next of kin."

"Call Rex." Lark hangs up the call, which switches her back to the incest phone line. Fergie is speaking.

"My mother had incest with me, okay? That's why I'm here, huh, like I'd be here if she didn't. Wouldn't hardly be hanging around with y'all unless I had to." Other phone callers laugh. "So I finally realized what my problem is. All my life I let people abuse me. I let my assistant push me around at work. I let bosses overwork me. My wife yells at me and hits me. My kids walk all over me. I'm ashamed of all the times I get taken advantage of by salespeople."

Klevon laughs quietly, nodding his head.

"Now I realize: that was abusive behavior. I was abused. I am abused. I'm infinitely abusable," Fergie says.

Pippi pats around for a pen. "Martha, get me a pen, hurry. I was abused. I am abused. What did he say?"

Martha hands her a pen. "Infinitely amusable."

"'I am infinitely amusable.' Is that right?"

"Ma'am, that's what I heard."

Fergie goes on. "When I heard someone else on the line telling the same story, my story, that was one eureka moment: ding-dong the bell! I'm not horribly flawed. I just have symptoms! Symptoms of childhood incest. Well, I won't be imprisoned by those symptoms anymore. I won't be taken advantage of. I've given up all contact with my birth family. I come to these meetings to be with my family of choice, my brothers and sisters, you. To listen to your solutions and have hope. I love you. I'm sorry. I pass."

Lark sits back down inside her closet hideaway. "Thanks, Fergie. Malea, can I share now? It's an emergency. It's Lark."

"Please share, Lark," Malea says.

"He's dying. My abuser is dying. I just got the phone call. They want me to come help him die. Ha-ha! I guess I could be kind. I could pretend he's just any old man dying. I would help a stranger. Diddly on that. He doesn't deserve kindness. But hey, maybe I can get him to apologize! A deathbed confession! That'd be worth a stab."

Another call beeps in. "That may be them calling again. I'll answer it. Thanks, everybody." Lark presses a phone button and switches to the other call.

"Hola."

"Lark, it's Georgia again. It won't be long now. Forgive and forget . . ."

Lark interrupts. "All right, I'll do it."

Georgia goes on as if she hasn't heard Lark. "Your mom's an old lady, like me. We need young people to . . ."

"I said I'd do it. I'll come."

"You will? Praise God."

"You could praise me instead, but whatever."

"That was a great line, Lark. Are you still writing? Bring some; I'd love to read it."

"I just might do that," Lark muses. "A eulogy maybe."

---

[1] Based on *Survivors of Incest Anonymous* script.

40

At Lark's childhood home, Lark's brother, Rex, now in his fifties, slumps in a recliner watching cartoons. Lark's seven-year-old niece, Dolores, is setting up dominoes in a circuitous route along the kitchen counter. Lark stands beside Scully's deathbed.

Like a child told to quit slouching, Hattie sits stiffly at the dining room table. Georgia slathers blue clay all over Hattie's face. Then Hattie covers Georgia's face with the blue clay. "You'll look ten years younger for the funeral," Georgia promises.

"Why would I want to do that?"

"Might meet a new man."

Hattie bursts out laughing. "That's the last thing I need."

"Now don't laugh," Georgia warns. "You'll crack. Pretend you're at the funeral."

"I'm not in a hurry to pretend when it's about to be real."

Rex wriggles in his chair. "It's not the kind of thing you practice for."

"Au contraire, mon frére!" says Lark. "Buddhists meditate on death all the time so they'll be ready when it comes, so they don't blow it."

Rex stands up. "How can you possibly blow death?"

"What you focus on while you're dying decides what happens to you in the next life," Lark explains. "Or something like that. I'm not a Buddhist."

"I would have pegged you for one."

"What do you mean by that?"

"Nothing. Just that you're all New Age, aren't you?"

"No."

Georgia joins the conversation. "I'm an animist. I believe that every living thing has a spirit. When I die, I'll become one with the universe."

Hattie laughs. "When it comes down to your own death, Georgia, I bet you'll be saying the Rosary."

"Might as well have all my holy cards stacked up, old girl, just in case."

"I have a good idea!" Hattie says. "I'll turn on the Rosary tape so Scully can listen to it while he's dying. Then he can slip straight into the arms of Mary the Virgin Mother. Isn't that how it works, Lark?"

Rex objects. "Why are you asking her? She's a heathen."

Hattie searches her audiotape collection and pulls out *The Rosary Chant* by Mother Angelica and the nuns of Our Lady of the Angels Monastery.

"Is that a cassette tape?" Rex takes it from Hattie. "I'll do it." Rex sets up the tape player on the dining room table and turns it on. Mother Angelica and the nuns begin praying the Lord's Prayer. "Our Father who art in heaven, hallowed be thy name. Thy kingdom come; thy will be done on earth as it is in heaven."

"Does it have to be so loud?" Lark complains.

Hattie says, "I want Daddy to hear it. You know he's practically deaf."

"Then put it over next to him, so we don't have to hear it."

"Heathen," Rex says. Pushing a bowl of applesauce aside,

Rex moves the tape recorder to Scully's hospital-issue bedside table. He plugs it into the extension pad, into which an oxygen apparatus and an IV drip are already plugged. Rex turns the recorder on again.

"Give us this day our daily bread and forgive us our trespasses as we forgive those who trespass against us . . ." Rex turns down the volume. The nuns recite the Rosary in the background.

Hattie toddles over to Scully's bed.

"Hattie! You're going to scare the life out of him with that blue face," Georgia warns.

"He'll think you're a demon carting him off to hell," says Lark.

Vying with the dying man for attention, Dolores takes a bow, then sings. "Ta-da! You are about to see the greatest, most incrediblest trick in the world, ever!"

"You going to raise the dead?" her dad asks.

"No."

"Because that would be the best trick in the world ever."

"Stop teasing her," Lark tells Rex. To Dolores she says, "Let's see your trick."

"I'm going to knock down one single domino, and the whole rest are gonna fall down all in a row."

"What if one refuses to fall down?" Lark asks.

Dolores says, "It doesn't have a choice."

"Dolores, don't be making noise," her dad says. "This isn't the time or place. It's disrespectful to your grandpa."

Dolores looks to Hattie, then to Lark, for support. "Oh, let her go ahead, Rex," Hattie says. "Scully will like it." She leans over Scully and shouts in his ear, "Look, dear, dominoes. You always played this game with Rex, remember?" To Dolores, she says, "Go ahead." Hattie turns Scully's face toward the little girl.

Dolores looks a question at her dad. Rex throws up his

hands. "Who am I to argue with Grandma?" Dolores flicks her finger against the first tile, and all the tiles fall dutifully one by one.

"Did you see that, dear?" Hattie asks Scully. "Just like Rex used to do."

Lark reminds Hattie, "I used to play that too."

"Did you?" Hattie asks. "I don't remember you."

To Lark, Dolores says, "I don't want him to die. I don't like dead people."

"How many dead people do you know?" Lark asks.

"I've watched zombie movies."

"You let her watch scary movies?" Lark objects to Rex. He shrugs.

"After my husband died," Georgia says, "I couldn't watch scary movies anymore. Death got to where it wasn't so amusing."

"And my cat got run over. Aunt Lark, Mom says cats go to heaven. Is that true?"

"I refuse to go to heaven if it's not."

Scully hiccups. "Look!" Hattie says. "He's laughing!"

Rex puts a hand on her shoulder. "It's just a reflex, Ma."

"They say the hearing's the last thing to go," Georgia points out.

"Is that so?" Lark asks.

"Yes," Georgia goes on. "I sat with Jonah reading a book out loud while he died."

"Was it his favorite book?"

"No, it was my favorite book."

Hattie stage-whispers to Lark, "Jonah was never much of a reader. More of a drinker. *Shhh.*"

"Say, that's a good idea," Georgia says. "I'll make us some Blue Moons to go with our blue faces. You have got gin, haven't you, Hattie? Of course you have." Georgia goes out to the kitchen.

"Rex, have you thought about what you're going to say at the funeral?" Hattie asks.

"Darnation, Momma," Rex whispers loudly, "he can still hear you!"

Georgia peeks her head in from the kitchen, a bottle of Bombay Sapphire gin in one hand. "How rude of me. Rex, would you like a Blue Moon? They're made with gin."

"Make it a double."

"Lark?"

"Not me. One day at a time."

"I just wanted you to remember some memories, Rex," Hattie says.

"I'd like to say a few words at the funeral, Momma," Lark announces.

Hattie pretends not to hear. She picks up a bowl of applesauce and a spoon from Scully's bedside table and urges Lark to take them. "Lark, feed him some applesauce." She baby-talks to Scully, "Him's hungwy, ithn't him?"

Hattie puts the bowl and spoon into Lark's hands. Georgia reenters from the kitchen holding a tray of blue cocktails. She offers one to Rex. He accepts it and drinks quickly. She doesn't offer one to Lark. She puts a drink in Hattie's hand.

"You're the mommy bird now, Lark. And he's da baby bird," Hattie says.

Georgia agrees, "That's what old age does."

When Lark moves into Scully's range of vision, he reaches for her, trying to rise in the bed. "Look, he knows who you are!" Hattie says with delight. Scully catches Lark's eye with his milky gaze and sucks with his mouth.

"He never remembered my name in his life. Be a miracle if

he could do it on his deathbed."

"Him knows who his onliest, loneliest daughter is, yes him does." Hattie reckons the urine level in Scully's catheter bag and gleefully reports, "More pee!"

"Leave the man to pee in peace a few minutes," Georgia says. "Time to wash off your blue face." Gripping the saggy flesh of her upper arm, Georgia drags Hattie toward the bathroom.

"No, but I have to . . ." Hattie protests.

"You need some 'you' time."

Hattie lays her head on Georgia's shoulder. "You're my oldest friend."

"I'm the oldest one still breathing."

Rex joins Lark at the deathbed. Dolores claims the recliner for her own. She calls loudly. "Is he dead yet? I want to go home."

Lark smiles like Ursula the mermaid witch, and forces applesauce into Scully's mouth. She coos, "Have some applesauce, Daddy. And a little arsenic. With curare." Scully chokes a little, then spits out the applesauce. It drips down his chin.

Rex pulls out a cigarette and puts it in his mouth unlit. "What would be the point of poisoning a dying man?"

"I'd be the one to kill him, not God."

"What's your problem with Dad, anyway? Contradicting solar signs? Bad chi?"

"You'll hear all about it in the eulogy."

"Mom wants me to give the eulogy," Rex reminds her.

"I'm the firstborn," Lark argues back.

"Well, I'm the man. And you know how Dad was. Is."

"A sexist piggie-wiggie?"

"You're a girl. He's an old-school Catholic. It would kill him if a female spoke at his funeral."

"Do you think? Hey, Dad!" Lark shouts into Scully's ear, "I'm gonna speak at your funeral." She watches Scully a moment, then says to Rex, "That didn't kill him. I'll have to try something else."

"Not funny, if that's what you're going for. Give him a break. He was a man of his time. Is."

"And his time's run out. I'm doing the eulogy."

"Cuckoo girl. The priest won't let you."

"What are you, stuck in the fifties? And call me 'woman,' boy.

Rex mimics his idea of a woman, "Hear me roar."

"Oh, you'll hear it, all right. Everyone will."

"What're you going to say?"

Lark sings, "Ding-dong, the old man's dead. The wicked old man. He's finally dead. Ding-dong, my wicked father's dead."

"Seriously."

"Him knows what I'm gonna say, doesn't him?" Lark speaks directly into Scully's face.

Rex looks worried. "What are you going to say, seriously?"

"Just a few words."

"Wait a minute. You tried to accuse Dad of something before. You're not going to bring that up again, are you? He denied it. I believed him. End of story."

"Not for me."

"This is just another one of your bipolar phases, isn't it, Lark the Dark? You're delusional again. You probably have a wet brain, what with your alcoholism."

"I'm sober ten years."

"No one will believe you! They'll remember your string of boyfriends. Your Druid period. You're not the stable one in this family."

"I'm surprised you left out my gambling problem. Then there's the bulimia."

"The priest has already been here. Dad confessed his sins, and God's forgiven him. Let him die in peace."

"God doesn't have the right to forgive him," Lark seethes. "Only I can forgive him." She shouts into Scully's ear, "And I don't! You never asked me for forgiveness." Lark puts down the applesauce and plays with Scully's oxygen tubing.

"It wasn't Dad. It was Glassman! He tried to kidnap you."

"No one was kidnapping anyone. I was running away." She raises her voice again and speaks to Scully. "From you!"

"It was a long time ago."

"I see it in my waking dreams as if it were yesterday."

"Give him a break. Everything isn't all about you. You you you. Think of someone else for a change."

"Me? Look who's talking, golden boy. Everything has always been about you you you." They both turn their heads at a knock on the front door.

41

Lark opens the door to reveal Carmen, the hospice nurse, dressed for the night of salsa dancing she's anticipating when her rounds are over: wearing spandex pants and spiked red heels. Her earrings are as big as her bracelets. Jangling and smelling like Gucci, she begins fussing over Scully.

"*Hola! Pura vida!* It's Carmen, your hospice nurse. Where's my man? Scully, you there? Can you hear me, Scully?" In an accent like Dracula, she says, "Look into my eyes. Hello. There you are." To Lark and Rex, she says, "He's still aware." After a bit more fussing, Carmen steps back from the bed to huddle quietly with the siblings.

"What's the prognosis?" Rex wants to know.

"*Shhh,* the hearing's the last thing to go. Even when they fall into a coma, they can still hear you. It won't be long now. Let me tell you what you're going to do to keep this quick and painless. Keep him warm, lots of blankets if he wants them. They tend to feel cold when the circulation stops. Don't give him any liquids. Stop foods, stop drugs, nothing by mouth. His digestive system is shutting down along with everything else, and it'll just send him off to his grave with a bellyache. We'll keep the oxygen flowing so he won't have to struggle for breath. His heart's just shutting down, so you

135

shouldn't face any deathbed antics. He'll just start to turn blue."

"You're making that up," Lark insists.

"No, *es la verdad*. It's true. He'll turn blue, then his heart will stop beating. *Voila*. An easy death. All my patients should be so lucky."

"We all should," says Rex.

"I'll just change his pee bag. Try to keep his hands off his doohickey. Don't let him pull the catheter out. His bladder could explode," Carmen warns.

"I know you're making that up," Lark says.

"You don't wanna find out. It's not going to be very long now. See the blue in his feet?"

"How long is very long now?" Rex asks.

"Hours? Minutes? Hard to say. Not very long." Carmen speaks into Scully's ear. "Scully, I'm going now. Just wanted to say *adios*, go with God. Have a safe journey to the other side." Carmen kisses Scully's forehead and hands Lark a business card. With salsa-wiggling hips, she high-steps out the front door, calling back over her shoulder, "Call me if you need anything. I do pet sitting."

Rex shuts the door behind Carmen and leans against it. "I'm not going to the funeral."

"Refusing to pay homage to the pedophile?"

"No. I'm staying to prevent you from going, Lark."

"You're going to hold me against my will, Rex? I'll charge you with kidnapping."

"Nobody will believe you. They'll think you're crazy. You are crazy."

"How do you suppose that happened? Huh?"

"You were born defective?"

"I think nurture beat out nature this time. I split off into another world when I was . . . when he . . . I had to. I couldn't stay where I was. I'd die."

"And you think that's the reason you're *loco*?"

"I do. I blame my mental illness on Daddy."

"There you go, always blaming other folks for your own faults."

"Since when is mental illness a fault?"

"Well, it's certainly not an asset," Rex says.

"Well, you certainly are an ass."

"Name calling is not conversation, Lark the Loon."

"Fustilarian."

"What the hell does that mean?"

"Takes a liberal arts degree to know."

"At least you went to college."

"No thanks to him. He told me girls didn't go to college. I had straight As, and he didn't let me apply anywhere."

"It was the times," Rex says.

Lark goes on. "I could have gotten into a good school! Instead, I ended up at junior college. He paid for your tuition. I had to foot the bill myself. It took me eight years, but I got a degree in spite of him."

"That's not my fault. What, did you want me to turn down my ride just to be fair? I wasn't a feminist."

"I can see why not. They made me be your servant: do your laundry, iron your school clothes, cook for you, and wash your dishes."

"They were training you to be a wife."

"I didn't want to be a wife. I wanted to be a writer."

"Count your blessings no one ever married you."

"Easier than counting your wives."

"Okay, so Mr. and Mrs. Psychopath ruined me too. It took me until my third wife to learn that a man ought to do some dishes."

"I still have nightmares about ironing your underwear."

"So you had it worse, okay? Is that what you want me to say?"

Lark shakes her head. "You don't have to say it. I'm doing the eulogy."

"What about Momma?" Rex asks. "What about Dolores?"

"It's Dolores I'm thinking of. It's all the children. They need to be protected from pedophiles."

"Please don't say that word. He's literally on his deathbed, Larkaholic. He can't abuse anyone anymore. You wouldn't be protecting Dolores; you'd be devastating her."

Lark whispers loudly into Scully's ear. "Yeah, you'll be dead soon, and then you'll rot in hell eternally. I'm looking forward to your funeral. Revenge is sweet."

"You're evil," Rex says.

"No, I'm not the one who's evil here. See any demons, Daddy?" She sings the old Dr. Demento song. "They're coming to take you away, ho hah, hee hee, ho hah."

"Dr. Demento. That's appropriate, demented one."

"Serial marry-er."

"Why can't you just get over it, Lark? It was a long time ago. From what I saw, he wasn't really hurting you." Rex is appalled to realize what he's just revealed.

"You saw?"

"I was just a little kid."

Reverting to the voice of a child, Lark says, "I was little too. Why didn't you do something?"

"What could I have done?"

"You could have told." Lark glares at Rex, who drops his gaze to the floor.

"Told what? How would I know anything was wrong with it? You were a girl. I thought it was normal for girls."

"It is normal. One out of four."

Dolores gets up from the TV chair and joins them at the bed. "What's one out of four?"

"Little pitchers have big ears," warns Rex.

"Like her Dumbo Daddy. Dolores, go ask Grandma if you can play with her jewelry. She'll let you."

"Goody goody," the little girl replies. She goes into Hattie's bedroom.

The siblings eye each other in silence. Finally, Rex says, "She washed my mouth out with soap."

"Who did?"

"Momma."

"For what?"

"For telling her."

Blue Moon in hand, Hattie walks in from the bedroom, the blue clay washed from her face. "Scully told me what he wanted to leave to people," she announces. "Rex, he wants you to have his videos and DVDs."

Rex looks through the DVDs and pulls one out.

"*The Mary Kate and Ashley Collection*?"

"They were some of his favorites. He always liked children."

"They were little girls, Momma, and he's a pedophile," Lark says. "But you know that, don't you?"

"Oh, Lark, you're always so dramatic," says Hattie.

"Oh, Momma, don't play oblivious with me," Lark answers back.

"Can't you ever be appropriate for once in your life?" Rex says between clenched teeth. "Her husband is dying."

"You knew, Momma! Rex told you Daddy was molesting me."

"I don't know what you're talking about."

"Tell her, Rex—you told her! You told me you told her. Tell her."

Rex says nothing. Hattie goes to Scully's bedside. Lark follows her.

"Oh, I almost forgot about you," Hattie tells Scully, "what with my drinking Blue Moons. How are you holding up, dear?"

"You knew," Lark says.

Georgia comes into the room. "Knew what?"

"That Daddy was molesting me. She knew."

"I knew?" Hattie finally says. "The world knew, the way you hussied around in your makeup and princess gowns. You made it quite clear what you were after."

"I was five years old."

"Always swishing around as if you had hips. Wearing makeup. You looked like a whore."

"He put that makeup on me."

"Don't you blame him for it. Men can only take so much invitation before they give in."

"Invitation? I was a little kid."

"Sitting on his lap. Making him carry you around like the silk slippers of the little princess couldn't touch the ground."

"I was his little princess."

"So you admit it now," Hattie says.

"Admit what? To being a little kid? About this high?" Lark lifts a framed photograph from the wall. "Look at this picture of me in kindergarten. Me and Daddy. He's holding me. Look how little I was!"

"Was that before or after your breakdown?" Rex butts in.

"What breakdown?" Hattie asks.

"You mean *which* breakdown, don't you, Momma?" Rex continues.

"I don't remember," Hattie says.

"You don't remember the year I stayed home from school?" Lark asks.

"You never did as well as your brother did. The nuns always said, 'Rex is so smart and such a good student. Lark never lives up to her potential.'"

"Do you remember my compulsive hand washing?" Lark asks.

Hattie hems and haws. "You seem to think I remember every little thing from way back then."

"I remember that," Rex says. "She was flipped out!"

"I had a psychotic break."

"You were delusional."

Hattie starts to say, "Rex, why don't you go . . ."

Lark interrupts. "Momma, you're dodging the question. How much did you know?"

"I honestly can't remember."

"You remember Daddy playing dominoes with Rex, but you don't remember Daddy raping me."

Hattie catches her foot on Scully's IV tube, trips and falls to the floor. Rex races over. "Are you all right?"

"*Oww!* I'm dying."

"Did you twist anything?" asks Rex.

"Hip hurts," Hattie tells him.

Georgia steps in and tries to help Hattie up. "Probably broken. Can you stand?"

"They say the hip goes first, and it's all downhill from there," Hattie moans.

"That's how it happened with Jonah," Georgia says.

Hattie wails, "Oh, it's the end of me."

"Don't be morose, Momma," Rex says. "It's just a little sprain."

"So now you're the doctor I wanted you to be? You're gonna tell me it's just a little sprain when the pain is about to kill me?"

"I'm taking you to the hospital," Rex announces.

"No, no. I'll be all right."

"Lark, help me," Rex says.

"No! Keep her away from me! Georgia, you help me."

"Where's Dad's wheelchair? We'll use that." Georgia and Rex help Hattie into the wheelchair.

Dolores comes out of the bedroom wearing Hattie's jewelry. "Where is everybody going?"

"I'm taking Gramma to the hospital," her father says. "You stay here with Aunt Lark."

"I wish it were my funeral instead of his," says Hattie. Georgia wraps Hattie up in the crocheted afghan from the sofa. Rex opens the front door and wheels Hattie out of the house.

Georgia pulls Lark aside. "Your mother sacrificed you to save the family. The family was everything."

"I was family too. She didn't save me."

"It was a different time. Husbands were gods, kings of their kingdoms. Wives obeyed. Didn't ask questions. Did what they were told."

"Doesn't sound much like my mother."

"Times are different now. Women's lib."

"Women's lib or not, one out of four girls is still sexually abused before she's eighteen," Lark tells Georgia. "That's why we have to talk about it."

"You can't talk about it. It'd kill your mom."

"Then she'll join her beloved in hell. I'm giving the eulogy."

"Why do you want to do this to her? What could she have done if she left? Women didn't just go and get jobs back then. It was a different time."

"It was my time. My life. Why did he matter more than me?"

"Because he was the man! Would you have had her living on the street with two little kids?"

"Yes! She should've fed us out of garbage cans instead of let him abuse me."

"She could have done that."

"But she didn't."

"No, she didn't," Georgia admits. "We all make mistakes in our lives. We're only human."

"He's not human. He's a fiend."

"He put food on your table and clothes on your back."

"Why are you defending him?"

"I'm not defending what he did to you. I'm just pointing out what he did *for* you. Jesus tells us to forgive our enemies, not for the sake of the enemy but for the sake of our own souls. Turn the other cheek."

"Jesus! Where was he when I was being raped by my own daddy?"

"You don't know the plans of God."

"I don't think any god plans to abuse children."

"I'm old. I'll die soon enough. Would you like to hear my daughters counting off my many sins at my funeral? It just isn't the place. It's too late for him to abuse any more children. Let it go. It's over."

Rex comes back into the house. "Georgia? She wants you to come with her."

"I'm tired. I'd rather go home to bed."

"Please, Georgia. She's getting hysterical out there. Thanks to Looney Bird."

"All right, I'm coming. Let me finish my drink." Rex goes back out.

Georgia puts her hand on Lark's shoulder. "Do everybody a big favor. Write a memoir. Give it to everyone to read. Or don't. Keep it under your pillow until you die. But don't ruin an old veteran's funeral. He'll get a military salute, you know."

"I hope they're pointing those rifles at his corpse."

"You have so much anger. It isn't doing you any good. Let it go, for your own sake."

Georgia goes out the front door. In the silence she leaves behind, Lark can hear the nuns on the cassette tape still chanting the Rosary.

"O my Jesus, forgive us our sins. Save us from the fires of hell. Lead all souls to heaven, especially those in most need of thy mercy."

42

Dolores sits at the kitchen counter, listlessly building domino houses. "I want to go home," the little girl whines.

"I'm sorry, Dolores," Lark says. "It's late for you. Let's tuck you in bed in your dad's old bedroom." They enter the bedroom that Lark once shared with Rex. Now it holds Lark's old bed and desk.

"I thought this was your bedroom," Dolores says.

Lark casts her thoughts back to her childhood. "No, it was your father's bedroom. My bedroom was in the attic."

"Daddy told me he switched bedrooms with you when you got sick, and he got the attic."

"Funny, I hardly remember that. But it's true. You're right."

"Can I see the attic?"

"The attic?" Lark thinks a moment, then says sharply, "No."

Dolores is taken aback by Lark's sudden anger. "Okay."

Lark cheers up. "Maybe some of my old toys are still here. Might as well look in that cupboard."

Lark opens a high cupboard door. Inside are Barbies. Lots of Barbies and a few Ken and Skipper dolls.

Dolores switches from being Eeyore to being Tigger. "Barbies!" Lark grabs a handful of Barbies and pulls them down from the cupboard. Dolores holds out her arms to catch them.

"I get Barbies when I've been a good girl," Dolores says. "You must've been a really good girl, Aunt Lark."

Dolores proceeds to take off all of the Barbie outfits until she has a pile of naked dolls. Then she picks her favorite Barbie and her favorite outfit and matches them up.

With the Barbies, a small box tied with twine falls out of the cupboard. Lark picks it up and sits on her old bed. She pulls the twine bow and opens the box. It's full of notes and letters. She unfolds a note and reads it.

Dear Glassman,
    I melted your glass. I'm sorry. Here it is.
    I hope you can still use the blob for something.
    I think it's pretty.
Yours truly,
Lark Kurvas

She reads through some of the other notes and clearly remembers writing them. "How did my letters to Glassman get here?" she asks out loud.

43

Later, Dolores is asleep. Lark turns off the bedroom light and comes out alone, then goes over to Scully's bed. "Daddy? Daddy, are you still alive? Wake up. I know you can hear me." She shakes Scully. He opens his eyes. "There. Look at me. Do you know who I am?"

Weakly, Scully guesses, "Mother?"

"Guess again."

Louder, yet feebly, Scully repeats, "Mother!"

"Momma's too busy to come. She sent me. No one here to help you. No one to protect you. From me."

"Robin?"

"You got it, Daddy-O. I'm your little girl."

"My little girl? No. She was . . . little."

"Just the way you like 'em. Little. Remember what you did to that little girl?"

"What? Nothing. No." Scully reaches up, trying unsuccessfully to grasp the overhead pull-up bar. Lark swats it out of his reach. It swings. She laughs.

"You're not my little girl. She loved me."

"Yes, she did. With all her tiny heart. You were her hero, her god. She'd do anything for you. Anything, huh, Daddy?"

"My little bird."

"She trusted you. And you betrayed her."

"Never."

"You did."

"Not."

"Don't give me that Alzheimer's. You remember. I know you do. How can you forget raping your daughter?"

"Mother! Mother!"

"I thought so. You remember all right. I'll remember until the day I die. And so will you. But you haven't got as long as I have. Your death is about to happen." Scully sputters. "Don't you die before I have time to kill you. You robbed me of my childhood. You're not going to rob me of my revenge." She rips the rosary beads out of Scully's hands and hangs them around her own neck. "Mary the Virgin Mother ain't comin' for to carry you home, Da-da." Lark moves to the front door and throws it open. Scully shivers.

"Cold, huh? Want me to close it? Tell me you're sorry, and I'll close the door."

Scully waves her away.

"This is your last taste of coolness, then, before you burn in hell." Lark whisks off the sheet and blanket covering Scully.

"A peaceful death. Why should you have one? A good, long life and an easy death. Why aren't you eaten away by cancer, suffering for your sins? Why aren't you syphilitic? Dying alone in the gutter? How do you rate a devoted wife while I'm alone? How come you lived to be eighty-goddamn-six? You should've died before you molested me. Why didn't God take you before? Why didn't the devil take you before you did that to me?"

Lark reaches for the oxygen tube. She kinks the tube a few times and lets it go. "Tell me you're sorry, or I'll turn off the oxygen."

Scully shakes his head. "No."

Lark pulls the oxygen nosepiece off Scully's face. "Answer me, because Carmen said if that catheter falls out, your bladder will explode. How's that for going out with a bang? All you have to do is say, 'I'm sorry,' and I'll leave the catheter alone."

Scully coughs, shaking his head and waving her away. She yanks the catheter out. Then she picks up the cup of water on the bedside table and pours it into Scully's mouth.

"Gulp gulp gulp. Satisfy your own thirst, that's all you ever did. Pig. I'll give you a stomachache to die for. How do you like that? All you have to do is admit what you did and apologize. Then I'll let you die in peace."

Scully chokes on the water. "Not so fast," Lark warns. "No, I want a lingering death. A suffering death. I want you to feel what it's like to hurt and hurt and hurt. Like me. I know hurt, so I can help you feel it too."

Scully manages to breathe out, "Stop. Please."

"You killed me first. You killed any joy in me, any hope to live a normal life. Now it's my turn. I'm going to murder your soul. Alexander Kurvas, Scully, for your sins against me, I damn you to hell. For all eternity. Satan's gonna love you. There's a special place in hell for pedophiles. Happy trails, Da-da. Carry that to your grave and rot in it."

Breathing in gulps, shivering, applesauce smearing his face, Scully keeps grabbing at the pull-up bar above him.

"Whatsa matter, Da-da? Seein' demons?"

"You. Demon."

"No, Daddy. Me innocent. You demon. Look, I see the devil. He's a comin' for you! Last chance to say you're sorry. Say you're sorry, and I'll give back the oxygen. Say you're sorry, and I'll chase the devil away. Say you're sorry, and I'll take back my curse. Maybe I'll even forgive you. Apologize for abusing me. That's all you have to do."

Scully falls back against his pillows. He breathes out two syllables, softly.

"What? What did you say? Did you say 'sorry'? Don't die now! Did you say you're sorry?"

His struggle for breath ceases. He's dead.

"Damn you to hell." She turns her back on him. She looks at her hands: they're shaking. She closes her eyes and takes a few deep breaths. Finally, she turns back to her father's body. She wipes the applesauce from her father's open mouth, then takes the rosary from her neck and puts it back into his hands. She picks up the sheet and blanket from the floor, shakes them out over Scully, then pulls them up over his face.

"I loved you. I was your little girl. You were my daddy. The man in my life. The big, giant man. My hero. I adored you. I adored you in spite of what you did. I thought it meant that you loved me, just like you said. Now look what you've done to me. Look what you've made of me now."

Lark closes the front door. As she turns back, she notices Dolores standing in the kitchen. They look at one another in a long silence.

Finally Dolores says, "Don't worry, Aunt Lark. I'm good at keeping secrets."

44

Later, Lark climbs up to her old attic room and sits by the window, illuminated by the moon. She calls in to the incest victims phone meeting, which has already begun. A young woman is speaking.

"So I decided I'd give up my baby for adoption. It wasn't its fault it was created by incest. It was innocent. When it, when he, was born, I walked away from him, never to return. That was my plan. But everywhere I look, I see a baby. And every baby I see, I wonder, is that him? I'm going mad. I can't do this. Thanks for listening. I pass."

Instantly, Lark speaks. "It's Lark. Please let me share next. It's an emergency again."

Malea tells Lark to go ahead.

"He's dead. My abuser is dead. He just died a minute ago. My heart is beating so hard. I didn't forgive him. I cursed him. Cursed his soul to burn in hell. I wish I believed in hell. I wish I believed that he'd pay for his crimes in the afterlife. I only believe that it's over for him now. No more suffering, no more joy. He never said he was sorry, but he did say something. Right as he was dying, he did say something, but I couldn't hear it. He whispered something."

Malea speaks up. "Lark, I believe he said he was sorry."

"Yeah, he said he was sorry," other phone callers on the line agree.

"Maybe. But I'm still gonna give the eulogy. Boy, they won't see it coming. Well, maybe my brother will. And my mom. But my dad's friends? Maybe some of them already know, but to those that don't, I'm gonna out him for the monster he is. *Was.* I'm glad he's dead. Can't wait for the funeral. You're all invited. Holy Innocents Catholic Church, Los Angeles. I'm going to give the greatest eulogy any incest victim ever delivered. I pass."

Fergie is on the line. "My condolences, Lark, or whatever I should say under these circumstances. Congratulations? Call me if you want to talk. I pass."

Louise jumps in. "It's Louise in Oregon."

"Go ahead, Louise," Malea says.

"I want to say, Lark, that I'm here if you need me. Call me. We'll talk more. I pass."

"I'm going to buy a tombstone," Lark says. "I'm going to have 'Dead Pedophile' carved on it. So anyone who ever goes to that cemetery and walks by his grave will know what he was. You don't think I'm still angry, do you? Not a little bit? I pass."

"Lark, it's Verena. I figured my anger would abate when my abuser died. It did, but not right away. Over time, I learned to express it in safe ways, to burn it off like karma."

"What's a safe way to burn it off?" Lark asks.

"I heard you mention a eulogy."

45

Rex, wearing black, and Lark, wearing red, stand outside the church door. "I've written the eulogy," Rex announces.

"Then there will be two," Lark quips.

"You're screwed up, Lark the Fart. Did you take your medication?"

"People have to know."

"No one has to know," Rex says.

"Someone has to tell."

"No, they don't."

"For Dolores. For all the children."

"You want to wreck Dolores's memory of her grandpa? And what about my other children? And their children. He's dead now. You can't hurt him any more than he's already hurt himself. He's rotting in hell. Be comforted by that. Why do you want to destroy his reputation?"

"Your reputation?"

"Okay, so my reputation too. And yours. Every family has its secrets. Let's just keep our little skeleton in the closet like everybody else. Think of the kids."

"I am thinking of the kids. Future kids. We've gotta talk about childhood incest or it'll just keep on."

"Don't say that ugly word. Okay, I agree, we'll talk about it.

We'll do a webinar. This just isn't the place."

Lark walks away from Rex and enters the church. Hattie sits in a wheelchair near the altar. Without glancing at the open casket, Lark steps into the front row with Georgia and Dolores. Rex joins them.

Mourners filter in, view the corpse, hug Hattie, pat Dolores on the head, shake hands with Rex, and try to hug Lark. Lark crosses her arms in front of herself, refusing hugs.

Mumbling in Latin, Father Mulcahy sprinkles holy water over Scully and his casket with a silver wand. Then an altar girl hands him a smoking censer of frankincense. Father Mulcahy swings it over and around the corpse. He gives the censer back to the altar girl and enters the pulpit. He makes the Sign of the Cross. Many of the mourners sign themselves as well. Father Mulcahy opens a large Bible and says:

> "A reading from the Book of Job.
> *Then Job answered, 'O that my words were written down!*
> *O that they were inscribed in a book!*
> *O that with an iron pen and with lead they were engraved*
> *on a rock forever!'*
> This is the word of the Lord."

The mourners murmur, "Thanks be to God."

Closing the Bible, Father Mulcahy addresses the room. "Friends, we are gathered here today to lay to rest the mortal remains of Scully Kurvas. Remember, these are only his remains. Scully himself, his eternal soul, has already gone to his reward. He's looking down on us and smiling now.

"Scully was active in our prayer ministry. A fervent Catholic all his life, baptized at birth, he took the Blessed Sacrament and was confirmed and married in the Church. I was able to give him the Last Rites before he died, absolving him of all his sins and guaranteeing his place in heaven. Still, we'll say the Rosary for him anyway, just in case. Before we begin to pray, would anyone like to say a few words about Scully? Please come forward."

Rex and Lark stand. Rex puts his hand on Lark's shoulder to push her down, then leaves the pew and walks up to the pulpit.

"My father. To many people, he was Scully. But to me, he was Dad. He taught me everything I know about how to be a man. About working for a living and supporting a family. Dad knew what was important. Spending time with the kids. Papa Scully, grandfather to my children.

"He loved to play. That may be what I remember best. He will be missed, but we celebrate that he's gone to his eternal reward. Thank you all for coming to pay respects to my dad, Scully Kurvas."

Rex leaves the pulpit. Both Lark and Georgia stand at the same time. Lark reluctantly gestures to Georgia to go first. Georgia climbs over Lark to exit the pew, then goes to the pulpit.

"I know a thing or two about Scully," Georgia starts. "He was my friend for six decades. I think I knew him pretty well. He wasn't perfect. He may yet do a stint in purgatory. But he was good to his wife, Hattie, my best friend. He supported her so she could stay home and raise her family. That's more than a lot of men do these days, pardon me for saying so.

"Scully wanted to be a priest when he was young, he told me once. But then he met Hattie, and, well, his fate was sealed. He had two beautiful children, Rex and Lark. And how many grandchildren?" She looks at Rex questioningly.

"Seven," Rex answers.

"Seven? My, you've been busy, Rex. Seven grandchildren. He loved kids. He was good to my kids, too, when they were growing up. He was like a kid himself, childlike and playful. He was a manly man too, though. He let Hattie wait on him hand and foot, I have to admit, but that was the way things were. They wanted it that way. It was her calling, and it was his.

"Hattie probably wishes I hadn't said that. Lord, am I rambling? I should have written something down, but I thought I would just wing it, you know? I guess I'm done now. No, let me add that Scully leaves behind his lovely wife of sixty-one years, Hattie. Wave, Hattie, so people can see you."

Hattie waves and pushes her wheelchair forward as Georgia leaves the pulpit. "I know the widow doesn't usually speak, but I'd like to say a few words. Scully would probably have a cow if he knew I was doing this. He was traditional. But he's in heaven now, and Scully, if you hear me, shut up. It's my turn to talk. Ha-ha.

"I met Scully when I was fifteen. He was twenty-five. He was the love of my life, all my life. Sixty-one years married. We had a party a year ago August. A lot of you were there. Sixty-one years. Who can believe that? That's a long time to wash up after one man. To be honest, I'm looking forward to fewer dishes and socks. But this is about him, not me. Sorry, Scul.

"People have been saying he was good with children, and he was. And by the way, Georgia, he died with his scapular on, which lets him skip purgatory, if you remember your catechism. But he was a good provider, too, and a generous husband. He gave me jewels. Jewels! 'For when I'm gone,' he said, 'in case you need money, you can sell 'em.' Well, now he's gone, and I'll be darned if I sell my jewelry. Sorry, Father. I'm sure I'm not long for this world, either, so I'm giving them all to my daughter, Lark. To remember him by. All the jewels, Lark. For you. And that's what I wanted to say. That's about all. I don't think anyone else is going to speak. Thank you all for coming and please join us at the house after the service for a little wake, a little whiskey. Scully would like that."

As Rex wheels Hattie back, Lark stands. Rex grabs her arm, trying not to make a scene. She shakes him off and goes to the pulpit.

"Hello, everyone. I'm Lark."

At the dimly-lit back of the chapel, Fergie, Louise, and Pippi from the phone line sit in a pew. Fergie stands. "Hi, Lark. I'm Fergie from Nevada." Lark looks at Fergie, confused.

Beside Fergie, Louise stands. "Louise from Oregon is here. Hi, Lark."

"Louise. You came," Lark marvels. "Fergie, you're here."

Pippi stands. "Hello, everyone. Great funeral. Hi, Lark! Nice to meet ya! Long flight. I like California. Let's do the beach."

"Hi, Pippi. Welcome," Lark says. "Welcome everybody!" She glances around the chapel to see if anyone else will stand, then looks at her handwritten eulogy.

"I'd like to say a few words about my father. My father was . . . my father was responsible for a lot of things in my life. He . . . my mom, my brother, and Mrs. O'Donnell already said a lot about my dad. I have nothing much to add, except one thing—one thing. My friends already know about that one thing. Pippi, Louise, Fergie." Lark takes a deep breath.

"My dad and I had secrets. I'll let him take them to the grave. For now. Save it for the memoir." Lark crumples up her eulogy, opens her father's dead hands and puts the paper into his fingers. Bending to Scully's ear, she whispers, "Look who's wearing lipstick now." She quietly leaves the church.

Dolores follows Lark outside. They sit on a bench in the churchyard.

"I don't like funerals," Dolores says. "I don't like dead people."

"I like some people better dead," Lark responds. They sit a few moments in silence. Fergie, Louise, and Pippi come out of the church and join them.

"Funerals are boring," Dolores says. "Let's play a game."

"Do you like games?" Fergie asks.

"I like games. Except don't tell. It's a secret. I don't like the game I have to play in the bathtub with Daddy."

The End

Incest. It's the ugliest word.

As common as cancer, and harder to cure.

Even with the world-changing #MeToo movement, childhood incest remains a taboo topic, especially among those who have survived it.

Let's lift the cone of silence and start talking about the sexual assault of children.

Please visit *The Ugliest Word* website for information on how to:

- Talk about it
- Recognize it
- Report it
- Prevent it

TheUgliestWord.com